The
Oldest Map
with the Name
America

❧

The
Oldest Map
with the Name
America

New and Selected Poems

Lucia Perillo

RANDOM HOUSE

NEW YORK

Some poems in this work have been published in *The Bellingham Review, The
Beloit Poetry Journal, The Black Warrior Review, Cimarron Review, Crazyhorse, Indiana
Review, Kenyon Review, Michigan Quarterly Review, The New Yorker, The Northwest Re-
view, Ploughshares, Quarterly West,* and *The Salt Hill Journal.*

Grateful acknowledgment is made to the following for permission to
reprint previously published material:

Northeastern University Press: Seven poems ("The Sweaters," "Landfill,"
"The News [A Manifesto]," "Dangerous Life," "First Job," "The North-
side at Seven," and "The Revelation") from *Dangerous Life* by Lucia Maria
Perillo. Copyright © 1989 by Lucia Maria Perillo. Reprinted by permis-
sion of Northeastern University Press.

Purdue University Press: Seventeen poems ("How Western Underwear Came
to Japan," "Skin," "The Body Mutinies," "Kilned," "On Belay," "Thinking
About Illness," "Women Who Sleep on Stones," "Limits," "What One Loves
Are Things That Fade," "Annunciation at a Foreign Film," "Tripe," "Com-
pulsory Travel," "The Roots of Pessimism," "Monorail," "Needles," "Cairn
for Future Travel," "The Body Rising") from *The Body Mutinies* by Lucia Per-
illo. Copyright © 1996 by Lucia Perillo. Reprinted from *The Body Mutinies*
with the permission of Purdue University Press for English-language distri-
butions only. All other rights reserved by Purdue University Press.

Library of Congress Cataloging-in-Publication Data

Perillo, Lucia Maria, 1958–
The oldest map with the name America : new and selected poems /
Lucia Perillo. — 1st ed.
p.   cm.
ISBN 0-375-50160-6
1. National characteristics, American—Poetry.   I. Title.
PS3566.E69146043   1999
811'.54—dc21   98-34561

The printing press could disseminate, but it could not retrieve. Waldseemüller himself learned the fantastic, irreversible reach of this new technology. When Waldseemüller changed his mind and decided that after all Amerigo Vespucci should not be credited as the true discoverer of the New World, it was too late . . . his map was already diffused in a thousand places and could not be recalled.

—DANIEL BOORSTIN, *The Discoverers*

Contents

PART ONE
From *Dangerous Life* (1989)

PART TWO
From *The Body Mutinies* (1996)

PART THREE
New Poems

Part One

⤬

FROM

Dangerous Life

(1989)

The Sweaters

Used to be, fellows would ask if you were married—
now they just want to know what kind of diseases
you've got. Mother, what did they teach you of the future
in those nun-tended schoolrooms of the Sacred Heart?

Nobody kept cars in the city. Maybe you'd snuggle
when the subway went dark, or take walks
down Castle Hill Avenue, until it ran into the Sound—
the place you called "The End": where, in late summer,

the weeds were rife with burrs, and tomatoes ripened
behind the sheds of the Italians, beside their half-built
skiffs. Out on the water,
bare-legged boys balanced on the gunwales
of those wooden boats, reeling in the silver-bellied fish
that twitched and flickered while the evening dimmed to purple.

What sweater did you wear to keep you from the chill wind
blowing down at The End, that evening you consented
to marry Father? The plain white mohair, or the gray
angora stitched with pearls around the collar?
Or the black cashmere, scoop-necked
and trimmed with golden braid, stored in a box below the bed
to keep it hidden from Grandma? Each one prized,
like a husband, in those lean years during the war.

I see him resting his face against whichever wool it was,
a pearl or a cable or braid imprinting his cheek
while the Sound washed in, crying *again, again.*

Mother, we've abandoned all our treasured things, your sweaters
long since fallen to the moths of bitter days. And what
will I inherit to soften this hard skin, to make love tender?

Landfill

The river was big water, and it swallowed me
the way it tried to swallow all the garbage they were driving
in, between the tracks and the river.
Bulldozers were forever pushing
humps of dirt into the greenish, muckish current,
shoring up the fill with clods of broken interstate.
Those humps became the home of rats

and two idle girls, choking on cigarettes,
come there to take the sacrament of pilfered wine.
As a bleary moon rose, she'd let the jeans drop from her waist,
clatter of glass from her hand and she dove,
naked, off the riprap. And I followed her
with clumsy strokes, into the September Hudson—
laying bets about which one of us would turn back first.

They say the river's poison now—
PCB. And you can walk further across it
than our skinny arms would ever carry us, without losing
dry ground. Today she's brought me back, the place
transformed into a park where mothers bring their healthy kids
for civilized, supervised play. The girls we were—
buried, with the freeway and the bottleglass, under a ball field . . .

girls who swam until their vision failed, woke
with the filthy water lapping their hair and a pink sun rising
over Mecca. And though I know she had the better stroke,
the years made me believe she gave in first—
filling up her restless life with home and child, a child
who shrieks when I touch him, as though he knows
I'm still out treading in the wave-lap: my hands could drag him under.

She pats my hand as though I were her other child,
maybe showing me how sometimes turning back is moving on.
Then she loads her boy into a swing
and pushes him away—away,
until his face becomes a blurring moon, blue eyes waxing
half in terror, half in the startled joy of free fall,
as he arcs the distance between here and those other days.

The News

(A Manifesto)

So today, yet another Guyanan will try to run the border
dressed in a dead housewife's hair—all they've recovered
since her disappearance from a downtown shopping mall.
An "incident," the paper says. Another "routine occurrence"—
wresting my trust ever further from the publicans
assigned to keeping us safe, whole. Rather:
vow to stay vigilant against the maiming
that waits hungry in each landscape, even in this
mundane procession of muddy spring days. To see
the tenacity of rooted hair for what it is:
an illusion as fleeting as courage. To keep the meat
between one's ribs from being torn, to keep the hard
marble of the cranium covered with its own skin.
To stay vigilant. To watch for signs of violence stirring
even in one's own machine. To keep both breasts
attached and undiseased. To keep the womb empty;
and yet to keep the organs living there
from shriveling like uneaten fruit, from turning
black and dropping. And not to mistake the danger
for a simple matter of whether or not
to put the body on the streets, of walking
or of staying home—; there are household cleansers
that can scar a woman deeper than a blade

or dumdum bullets. The kitchen drawers are full of tools
that lie unchaperoned. Even with the doors and windows
bolted, in the safety of my bed, I am haunted by the sound
of him (her, it, them) stalking the hallway,
his long tongue already primed with Pavlovian drool.
Or him waiting in the urine-soaked garages of this city's
leading department stores, waiting to deliver up the kiss
of a gunshot, the blunted kiss of a simple length of pipe.
But of course I mean a woman's larger fear: the kiss
of amputation, the therapeutic kiss of cobalt.
The kiss of a deformed child. Of briefcase efficiency
and the forty-hour workweek. Of the tract home:
the kiss of automatic garage-door openers that
despite the dropped eyelid of their descent do nothing
to bar a terror needing no window for entry:
it resides within. And where do we turn for protection
from our selves? My mother, for example, recommends marriage—
to a physician or some other wealthy healer. Of course
it's him, leering from his station behind her shoulder,
who's making her say such things: the witch doctor,
headhunter, the corporate shaman, his scalpel
drawn & ready, my scalp his ticket out.

Dangerous Life

I quit med school when I found out the stiff they gave me
had Book Nine of *Paradise Lost* and the lyrics
to "Louie, Louie" tattooed on her thighs.

That morning as the wind was mowing
little ladies on a street below, I touched a Bunsen burner
to the Girl Scout sash whose badges were the measure of my worth:

Careers . . .
Cookery, Seamstress . . .
and *Baby Maker . . .* all gone up in smoke.

But I kept the merit badge marked *Dangerous Life,*
for which, if you remember, the girls were taken to the woods
and taught the mechanics of fire,

around which they had us dance with pointed sticks
lashed into crucifixes that we'd wrapped with yarn and wore
on lanyards round our necks, calling them our "Eyes of God."

Now my mother calls the pay phone outside my walk-up, raving
about what people think of a woman—thirty, unsettled,
living on food stamps, coin-op Laundromats & public clinics.

Some nights I take my lanyards from their shoebox, practice baying those old camp songs to the moon. And remember how they told us that a smart girl could find her way out of anywhere, alive.

First Job/Seventeen

Gambelli's waitresses sometimes got down on their knes,
searching for coins dropped into the carpet—
hair coiled stiff, lips coated in that hennaed shade of red,
the banner-color for lives spent in the wake of husbands
dying without pensions, their bodies used in ceaseless
marching toward the kitchen's dim mouth, firm legs
migrating slowly ankleward. From that kitchen doorway,
Frankie Gambelli would sic a booze-eye on them,
his arms flapping in an earthbound pantomime of that
other Frank: The Swooned-Over. "You old cunts,"
he'd mutter. "Why do I put up with you old cunts?"—
never managing to purge his voice's tenor note
of longing. At me—the summer girl—he'd only stare
from between his collapsing red lids, eyes that were empty.

Once I got stiffed on a check when a man jerked crazy-faced
out of his seat, craned around, then bolted
from those subterranean women, sweaty and crippled
in the knees. Though I chased him up the stairs to the street,
the light outside was blinding and I lost the bastard
to that whiteness, and I betrayed myself with tears.
But coming back downstairs my eyes dried on another vision:
I saw that the dusk trapped by the restaurant's plastic greenery
was really some residual light of that brilliance happening
above us on the street. Then for a moment the waitresses

hung frozen in midstride—cork trays outstretched—
like wide-armed, reeling dancers, the whole
some humming and benevolent machine that knew no past, no future—
only balanced glasses, and the good coin in the pocket.
Sinatra was singing "Jealous Lover." All of us were young.

The Northside at Seven

Gray sulfurous light, having risen early this morning
in the west, over the stacks of Solvay, has by now
wafted across the lake and landed here on Lodi Street,
where it anoints each particular with the general grace
of decay: the staggering row houses, the magazines flapping
from the gutters like broken skin, the red Dodge sedan
parked across the street from where I'm hunched in the pickup.
The Dodge's driver was ahead of me at the counter
in Ragusa's Bakery, making confession before an old woman
who was filling pastry shells with sweetened ricotta:

I put a new roof on her house, he was telling the woman,
but the lady don't pay me. I do a good job; she got no complaint.
But see, a man must hold his head high so I took her car.
The old woman trilled as she stuffed another log of cannoli.
Turning to me he said, *She can call the cops if she wants——*
I'll tell'em I got kids to take care of, I got a contract.
I shrugged: all the absolution I could bring myself to deliver
before grabbing the white paper sacks the woman slapped down
and walking out the door, leaving the man in the midst
of what he needed to say. I don't know——

there was something about his Sicilian features, his accent,
his whole goddamned hard-luck story that just gnawed on me so,
like those guys who came to unload on my own old man, muttering

Bobby, Bobby, see we got a little problem here Bobby . . .
the cue for women, kids to leave the room. But since then
my father has tried to draw me back into that room,
driving me along the tattered Bronx streets of his boyhood,
sometimes lifting his hands from the steering wheel and
spreading them, saying: *Look, these people are* paesan,
you're paesan, *nothing you're ever gonna do can change that* . . .

We'd spend the rest of the day on food, eating spiedini,
the anchovy sauce quenching my chronic thirst
for salt, and shopping for the dense bread made from black
tailings of prosciutto, I forget the name of it now.
I forget so much. I even forget why tears come on the freeway,
mornings I drive by these old buildings when bread is cooking—
why? for what? Sometimes I feel history slipping from my body
like a guilty bone, & the only way to call it back
is to slump here behind the wheel, licking sugar from my chin,
right hand warmed by the semolina loaves riding shotgun,

the way my father might have spent his early mornings years ago,
before he claimed the responsibilities of manhood—of marrying
and making himself a daughter who would not be trapped, as he
felt he was, by streets washed over in the slow decay of light.
Making her different from what he was. And making her the same.

The Revelation

I hit Tonopah at sunset,
just when the billboards advertising the legal brothels
turn dun-colored as the sun lies
down behind the strip mine.

And the whores were in the Safeway,
buying frozen foods and Cokes
for the sitters before their evening shifts.
Yes they gave excuses to cut
ahead of me in line, probably wrote bad checks,
but still they were lovely at that hour,
their hair newly washed
and raveling. If you follow
any of the fallen far enough
—the idolaters, the thieves and liars—
you will find that beauty, a cataclysmic
beauty rising off the face of the burning landscape
just before the appearance of the beast, the beauty
that is the flower of our dying into another life.
Like a Möbius strip: you go round once
and you come out on the other side.
There is no alpha, no omega,
no beginning and no end.

Only the ceaseless swell
and fall of sunlight on those rusted hills.
Watch the way brilliance turns
on darkness. How can any of us be damned.

Part Two

❧

The Body Mutinies

(1996)

How Western Underwear
Came to Japan

When Tokyo's Shirokiya Drygoods caught fire
in the thirties, shopgirls tore the shelves' kimonos
and knotted them in ropes. Older women used
both hands, descending safely from the highest floors
though their underskirts flew up around their hips.

The crowded street saw everything beneath—
ankles, knees, the purple flanges of their sex.
Versus the younger girls' careful keeping
one hand pinned against their skirts, against
the nothing under them and their silk falling.

$Skin$

Back then it seemed that wherever a girl took off her clothes
    the police would find her—
in the backs of cars or beside the dark night ponds, opening
    like a green leaf across
some boy's knees, the skin so white and taut beneath the moon
    it was almost too terrible,
too beautiful to look at, a tinderbox, though she did not know.
    But the men who came
beating the night rushes with their flashlights and thighs—
    they knew. About Helen,
about how a body could cause the fall of Troy and the death
    of a perfectly good king.
So they read the boy his rights and shoved him spread-legged
    against the car
while the girl hopped barefoot on the asphalt, cloaked
    in a wool rescue blanket.
Or sometimes girls fled so their fathers wouldn't hit them,
    their white legs flashing as they ran.
And the boys were handcuffed just until their wrists had welts
    and let off half a block from home.

God for how many years did I believe there were truly laws
    against such things,
laws of adulthood: no yelling out of cars in traffic tunnels,
    no walking without shoes,

no singing any foolish songs in public places. Or else
     they could lock you in jail
or, as good as condemning you to death, tell both your lower-
     and upper-case Catholic fathers.
And out of all these crimes, unveiling the body was of course
     the worst, as though something
about the skin's phosphorescence, its surface as velvet as
     a deer's new horn,
could drive not only men but civilization mad, could lead us
     to unspeakable cruelties.
There were elders who from experience understood these things
     much better than we.
And it's true: remembering I had that kind of skin does drive me
     half-crazy with loss.
Skin like the spathe of a broad white lily
     on the first morning it unfurls.

The Body Mutinies

—outside Saint Pete's

When the doctor runs out of words and still
I won't leave, he latches my shoulder and
steers me out doors. Where I see his blurred hand,
through the milk glass, flapping good-bye like a sail
(& me not griefstruck yet but still amazed: how
words and names—medicine's blunt instruments—
undid me. And the seconds, the half-seconds
it took for him to say those words). For now,
I'll just stand in the courtyard, watching bodies
weave into then out of one lean shadow
a tall fir lays across the wet flagstones.
Before the sun clears the valance of gray trees
and finds the surgical-supply shop's window
and makes the dusty bedpans glint like coins.

Kilned

I was trying somehow to keep [my early pieces] true to their nature, to allow the crudeness to be their beauty. Now I want the lava to teach me what it does best.

—STEPHEN LANG

These days when my legs twitch like hounds under the sheets
and the eyes are troubled by a drifting fleck—
I think of him: the artist
who climbs into the lava runs at Kalapana,
the only person who has not fled from town
fearing the advance of basalt tongues.
He wears no special boots, no special clothes,
no special breather mask to save him
from poison fumes. And it is hot, so hot
the sweat drenches him and shreds his clothes
as he bends to plunge his shovel
where the earth's bile has found its way to surface.
When he catches fire, he'll roll in a patch of moss
then simply rise and carry on. He will scoop
this pahoehoe, he will think of Pompeii
and the bodies torqued in final grotesque poses.
Locals cannot haul away their wooden churches fast enough,
they call this the wrath of Madame Pele,
the curse of a life that was so good

they should have known to meet it with suspicion.
But this man steps into the dawn and its yellow flames,
spins each iridescent blue clod in the air
before spreading it on a smooth rock ledge for study.
First he tries to see what this catastrophe is saying.
Then, with a trowel in his sweaty, broiling hand,
he works to sculpt it into something human.

On Belay

Should we fall, we've got protection:
hex bolts jammed into the cracked face of this rock.
I play out rope as you climb, your shoulder-blade bones
punching at the female contours of your back.
Truth is, you're not too good yet at this sport
where no move can be recalled or done again.
So you warn me not to tell you if
the chocks pop out, and I don't, I just watch them
shuttle down the rope to clang against what holds.
I'm thinking of your mother, Rose,
in her New Jersey kitchen making gravy:
what she would say now if she saw you here,
one finger's breadth away from falling
and bashing out your brains against these rocks.
What she wanted for you most
was protection: a lawyer husband, your hair
made a helmet the first Thursday of every month,
a son named Anthony or Francis. She rakes her fingers
against her throat, mouths one fricative oath
before she throws another pork bone in the pot.
I look up to see you hanging by one arm
and wonder what good this rope can do us, now
that your mother has sworn all twelve sides of the dice
are painted black: Sylvio's bypass, the world
gone to hell in a basket and what we hold to

just a temporary ledge. But isn't that why
we've come here after all, to waver on the seam
between this life and nothing, like love's
clenched fist, like the egg that each month zippers off
the milky surface of the ovary, before
its downward spiral, its sidereal crash and burn?
And we're already goners, should we fall or not.

Thinking About Illness
After Reading About
Tennessee Fainting Goats

Maybe they're brethren, these beasts bred clumsy,
hobbling stiff-legged over cheatgrass tufts.
Prized for how they'll freeze unpredictably
then fall, rehearsing their overwrought deaths.
Sometimes it's the woman who brings the meal
who sets them off by wearing yellow slacks,
or sometimes the drumming a certain wheel
makes on the road's washboard. Stopped in their tracks
they go down like drunks: Daisy and Willow
drop always in tandem, while Boot will lean
his fat side first against the hog-hut door.
How cruel, gripes a friend. But maybe they show
us what the body's darker fortunes mean—
we break, we rise. We do what we're here for.

Women Who Sleep

on Stones

Women who sleep on stones are like
brick houses that squat alone in cornfields.
They look weatherworn, solid, dusty,
torn screens sloughing from the window frames.
But at dusk a second-story light is always burning.

Used to be I loved nothing more
than spreading my blanket on high granite ledges
that collect good water in their hollows.
Stars came close without the trees
staring and rustling like damp underthings.

But doesn't the body foil what it loves best?
Now my hips creak and their blades are tender.
I can't rest on my back for fear of exposing
my gut to night creatures who might come along
and rip it open with a beak or hoof.

And if I sleep on my belly, pinning it down,
my breasts start puling like baby pigs
trapped under their slab of torpid mother.
Dark passes as I shift from side to side
to side, the blood pooling just above the bone.

Women who sleep on stones don't sleep.
They see the stars moving, the sunrise, the gnats
rising like a hairnet lifted from a waitress's head.
The next day they're sore all over and glad
for the ache: that's how stubborn they are.

$L\,i\,m\,i\,t\,s$

The dead man.
Every now and again, I see him.
And the wildlife refuge where I worked then,
the shallow ponds of Leslie Salt Company
patchworking the San Francisco Bay edges
and spreading below the hills like broken tiles,
each pond a different color—from blue to green
to yellow until finally the burnished red
of terra cotta, as the water grew denser
and denser with salt. Dunlins blew upward
like paper scraps torn from a single sheet,
clouds of birds purling in sunlight, harboring
the secret of escaped collision. And
that other miracle: how these weightless tufts
could make it halfway to Tierra del Fuego
and back before spring's first good day.
On those good days, a group from the charity ward
named after the state's last concession to saints
would trudge up the hill to the visitor center,
where I'd show them California shorebirds
—a stuffed egret, western sandpiper and avocet
whose feathers were matted and worn to shafts
from years of being stroked like puppies.
As I guided their hands over the pelts
questions stood on my tongue—mostly

about what led them to this peculiar life,
its days parceled into field trips
and visits to the library for picture books
with nurses whose enthusiasms were always greater
than their own. Their own had stalled out
before reaching the moist surface of their eyes,
some of the patients fitting pigeonholes built
in my head, like *Down's syndrome* and *hydrocephaly.*
But others were not marked in any way,
and their illnesses cut closer to the bones
under my burnt-sienna ranger uniform.
Maybe I was foolish to believe in escape
from the future foretold by their uncreased palms:
our lives overseen by the strict, big-breasted nurse
who is our health or our debts or even
our children, the *her* who is always putting crayons
and lumps of clay in our hands, insisting
we make our lives into some crude but useful thing.
And one day a man, a patient who must have been
supervised by his strict heart, fell down
suddenly and hard, on his way up the hill.
Two nurses prodded him on toward the building,
where he went down again like a duffel full of earth
in front of the reception desk where I was sitting.
I watched the one male nurse turn pale as ash
when he knelt to certify the heartbeat
of this man whose lips were blue and wet.
The other nurse took the group to the auditorium,
saying *James isn't feeling very well right now.*
James is sick. Get away from him. Then I heard
the dopey music of the automated slide show
behind those doors from which she never reappeared.
The male nurse was too young to leave stranded
with a man down on the smooth wood floor:

his cheeks still velvet, his dark fingers
worrying the valleys of the man's white wrist.
He's okay, he's breathing, as the man's skin
turned the same gray slapped on the hulls of ships,
his mouth open, a cherry sore at either edge.
I don't remember what I did at first,
I must have puttered off to perform some
stupid task that would seem useful—
gathering premoistened towelettes
or picking up the phone while the nurse repeated
He's okay, he's breathing. But the colors
got worse until nothing could spare me
from having to walk my hand in the crease
of the man's blue throat, where his carotid
should have pulsed. Nothing.
Must have just quit, the male nurse said.
I said *You breathe for him and I'll compress,*
and for a while we worked together like a clumsy
railroad handcar, me humping at arm's length
over the ribs, the nurse sealing his lips around
the man's scabbed mouth, while yellow mucus
drained from James's eyes and nose and throat.
Each time the nurse pressed his mouth to the man's
like a reluctant lover, the stink of cud
was on his lips when he lifted up. Sometimes
he had to hold his face out to the side,
to catch a few breaths of good salt air.
Until he was no longer able to choke back his gut
and asked if I would trade places with him.
For a minute I studied the man's stoved chest
which even my small knuckles had banged to jelly,
then the yellow pulp that flecked the nurse's lips,
that sour, raw smell from their mix of spit.
And I said: *No. I don't think I could . . .*

It's strange what we do with the dead
—burning them or burying them in earth—
when the body always tries to revert to water.
Later, a doctor called to say the man's heart
had exploded like a paper sack: death hooked him
before he even hit the floor. So everything we did
was useless—we might as well have banged a drum
and blown into a horn. And notice how I just said "we"—
as though the nurse and I had somehow married
spirits in a pact of gambled blood, when in truth
the nurse, like the man, rode off in an ambulance,
the man for a pointless go-round in the ER, the nurse
for a shot of gamma-globulin, while I stood
in the parking lot, picking lint off my shirt.
End of story. Except that since then James
has followed me, sometimes showing up at the house
to read my gas meter, sometimes behind the counter
where I ask him what I owe. No surprise then
that I've made my life with another James,
who swears my biggest defect is still the limits
on what I'll bring myself to do for someone else.
I know there are people who'll cut out their kidney
to replace a friend's cankered one, people
who'll rush into burning buildings to save the lives
of strangers. But every time I ponder selflessness
I hear the beats of my heart, that common loon,
most primitive of birds. Then life seems most
like a naked, frail thing that must be protected,
and I have suddenly become its mother, paddling
furiously with my own life saddled on my back.
There's one last thing I didn't mention—
when I refused to breathe for the dying James

what happened next was that I began to laugh:
a thin laugh, nervous laugh . . . but loud enough
to drift outside, where it stood on the hill
and creaked its wings a minute before lifting—
over the levees, across those shallowest of waters.

"What One Loves Are Things That Fade"

No matter how sweetly it begins, not long
into lovemaking I will see their faces—
there but not there, like creatures inseparable
from the dusk that stirs them to the clearing.
This time, it's the nuns who were forced
off the road near Santa Ana: camp shirts
disheveled round their necks, their fingers
tangled with the amber rosaries and
concussive gunfire of the tropics.
Ghosts that come stippled by the TV news
beamed down so relentlessly from space.
Ghosts of the Wirephoto, ghosts of the biopic,
ghosts that sometimes arrive incarnate
like the risen dead. Like the woman I dined with
who parted her hair during the coffee and sweets
to show me the trench knocked into her skull
with a brick. She couldn't remember a thing,
not what he looked like or how his hands felt
on her skin. But surely what was struck
from the broken slate of her included this:
quick breaths in the face and the body spinning
down its own dark shaft. How loud the queue

of women gathered at the doorjamb, clamoring
to braid themselves into that falling.
And after they go, worse, the spotlit quiet—
when comes the cry that I swear isn't mine.

Annunciation

at a Foreign Film

Friday night at the odeum and I'm surrounded by ghosts
like these three girls lighting on the row ahead.
They're homing in on darkness's momentum,
snapping gum and sucking out its pith.
By turns they're also swigging from a juice jar,
jigging their wrists to make the ice cubes clink,

and in that ill-tempered chiming I remember
the jar and the thermos and tangerines vodka-spiked
with a needle, courtesy of someone's diabetic dad.
How the juice burned running down my throat.
How I pitched my voice a half-shriek higher
so that it spiraled overhead. Soon as it's dark

you can bet on them burying the Italian bombshell
with their snickers: they're not about
to let themselves be cowed by someone else's babe.
But by then I'll be unspooling reels inside my head
and carrying these girls piggyback like wings,
back to days before the theater's conversion—

ornate cornices gone multiplex and carpet run up
on the walls. Here in the balcony—now gutted

and boxed—we were the virgins broadcasting
from heaven, fallout from the coned projector light
dusting our skin while everybody pitted down below
made only quiet, bovine vespers. Sophia Loren

pillaged in the subtitles was nothing
enough to make me flinch, except when her breast
appeared onscreen in such extravagant diameter
it made me want to stay buzzed forever, me
who imagined herself loud but never *that* conspicuous.
I needn't have worried: screens pretty soon

dwindled, and there were enough pinhead-scale angels
conspiring to keep me small as dust. And this
is what I'd warn the shrillest girl about
when my fingers tap her shoulder's leather slope.
But the message comes out a hissing sound, the words
having drained for so many years through my clenched teeth.

Tripe

We were never a family given to tongue or brains.
So the cow's stomach had to bear her last straws,
had to be my mother's warning-bell that chops and roasts
and the parched breasts of chickens, the ribs and legs
and steaks and fish and even the calf's sour liver
had become testaments to the monotony of days.
Since then I have understood the rebellion hedged
in its bifurcated rind, its pallor, its refusal
to tear or shred when chewed on by first
the right then the left jaw's teeth—
until finally the wad must be swallowed whole.

The tough meat meant life's repertoire had shrunk
to a sack inside of which she was boxing shadows—
kids and laundry, yes, but every night the damned
insistence of dinner. And wasn't the stomach
a master alchemist: grass and slops and the green dirt
transformed into other cuts of bloody, marbled beef.
Times when she wanted her own transformation
the house filled with its stewing, a ghastly sweet
that drove us underneath the beds. From there
we weathered the bomb-clouds rising off her range,
blowing the kitchen walls as wide as both Dakotas.

And I pictured her pale-faced & lustrous with steam
as she stood in that new open space, lifting
the hair off her neck as the stockpot billowed
its sugary haze like the sweat of a hired man.

Compulsory Travel

Not yet did we have personalities to interfere
with what we were: two sisters, two brothers.
Maybe our parents really were people who walked in the world,
were mean or kind, but you'd have to prove it to us.
They were the keepers of money, the signers of report cards,
the drivers of cars. We had a station wagon.
Back home we even had a dog, who was fed
by a neighbor kid while we toured the Jersey shore.
We waded in the motel pool and clung
to the edge of the deep end, because we couldn't swim.
Maybe that's why we never went in the ocean, despite
hours of driving. We could've just gone down the block!
Yet each year we made a ritual of this week
spent yelling and cursing and swatting each other,
with none of the analyses we now employ, the past
used as ammunition, the glosses from our latest therapist.
Back then a sock in the jaw could set anyone straight.

On Sunday afternoon, the homeward traffic would grind still
where the turnpike bottlenecked. My father
would slam his forehead against the steering wheel,
start changing lanes and leaning on the horn.
Without breeze through the window, the car would hold
our body heat like an iron skillet, skin peeling
from our burned shoulders as we hurled pretzels

and gave the finger to kids stopped in cars beside us.
My mother wouldn't mention the turn we'd missed
a few miles back; instead she'd fold the map
and jam it resolutely in the glove box while we crept on.
Perhaps this was our finest hour, as the people
we were becoming took shape and began to emerge:
the honkers of horns and the givers of fingers.
After the sun turned red and disappeared, we rolled
through darkness, wondering if the world knew all its names:
Wickatunk, Colts Neck, Zarephath, Spotswood—in every town
there were houses, in every house a light.

The Roots of
Pessimism in Model Rocketry,
the Fallacy of Its Premise

X-Ray had a see-thru payload chamber.
The Flying Saucer model was a gyp—
unless you were the kind of kid who loved
the balsa wood shredding more than airtime,
the smashing down more than the going up.
When Big Bertha sheared my brother's pinkie
I watched medicine make its promise good:
in the future we would all be androids.
The doctors reinstalled his milky nail
and drained blue fingertip, though afterward
I felt a little cheated. Already
I'd envisioned how his mutant terrors
could be put to my use, the naked stub
unsheathed to jinx an enemy's sneaker.

We were a tribe of Josef Mengeles
doing frontier science: putting crickets
in the payload, betting if they'd return
alive or dead. I always bet on death
because they always came down dead, I was
the pessimist, the child of many coins.

When someone fished from the dusty ballfield
the cocktail sausage of my brother's loss,
I gave its odds less than even money.
My vote was Put the finger in a can,
send it to Estes Model Rocket Co.
who would feel guilty enough to send cash.
But guilt turned on me. Now my brother's hand
looks perfect, except when he makes a fist.

Monorail

—*Seattle, at the old World's Fair*

He stands by the helm, his face full of blue
from the buildings at twilight, his hand
knuckled around a metal pole that will keep him
from falling, when he flies past the vaults
of startled mannequins, the red ohs of their lips.
Christmas lights are also falling
through the windshield, onto his chest:
right side green, left side red—
dark then back again.

But wait . . . my father is not moving yet;
no pilot has claimed the worn leather throne.
But his thoughts *are* moving, wondering
if movement is the same as growing old
in the province of space, not time. Inside his shoes,
his toes are as blue as the city streets,
and the drum in his chest, his red-lit chest,
is growing dim. He knows the train he's about to ride
has one rail: no steering, no turns.
And the only skill is in the brake.

The brake. His lips roll over the words:
the dead-man's brake. And a small boy
—come to ride up front—hears him,
tugs my father's coat and asks:
Hey mister, are you the driver of this train?

Needles

So first there's the chemo: three sticks, once a week,
    twenty-six weeks.
Then you add interferon: one stick, three times a week,
    forever.
And then there's the blood tests. How many blood tests?
    (Too many to count.)
Add all the sticks up and they come down to this: either
    you're coming out clean
or else . . . well, nobody's talking
    about the B side,
an *or else* that plows through your life like a combine
    driven at stock-car speed,
shucking the past into two piles: *things that mattered*
    and *things that didn't.*
And the first pile looks so small when you think of
    everything you haven't done—
never seeing the Serengeti or Graceland, never running
    with the bulls in Spain.
Not to mention all the women you haven't done yet!—
    and double that number of breasts.
Okay—
    you've got a woman, a good woman, make no mistake.
But how come you get just one woman when you're getting
    many lifetime's worth of sticks?
Where was the justice in that? You feel like someone
    who's run out of clean clothes

with laundry day still half a week away; all those women
    you tossed in the pile
marked *things that didn't matter,* now you can't help but
    drag them out.
Like the blonde on trail crew who lugged the chainsaw
    on her shoulder up a mountain
and bucked up chunks of blighted trees—how could you
    have forgotten
how her arms quaked when the saw whined and the muscles
    went liquid in her quads,
or the sweaty patch on her chest where a mosaic formed
    of shiny flies and moss?
Or that swarthy-haired dancer, her underpants hooked
    across her face like the Lone Ranger,
the one your friends paid to come to the table, where
    she pawed and made you blush:
How come yer getting married when you could be muff-diving
    every night?
At college they swore it was John Dewey, they swore
    by the quadruped Rousseau,
and it took cancer to step up and punch your gut
    before you figured:
that all along immortal truth's one best embodiment
    was just
some sixteen-year-old table-dancing on a forged ID
    at Ponders Corners.
You should have bought a red sports car, skimmed it under
    pale descending arms at the railroad crossing,
the blonde and brunette beside you under its moon-roof
    & everything smelling of leather—
yes yes—this has been your flaw: how you have always
    turned away from the moment
your life was about to be stripped so the bone of it
    lay bare and glittering.

You even tried wearing a White Sox cap to bed but its bill
        nearly put your wife's eye out.
So now you're left no choice but going capless, scarred;
        you must stand erect;
you must unveil yourself as a bald man in that most
        treacherous darkness.
You remember the first night your parents left town, left
        you home without a sitter.
Two friends came over and one of them drove the Mercury
        your dad had parked stalwartly
in the drive (you didn't know how yet):—took it down
        to some skinny junkie's place
in Wicker Park, cousin of a friend of a cousin, friend
        of a cousin of a friend,
what did it matter but that his name was Sczabo.
        Sczabo!—
as though this guy were a skin disease, or a magician
        about to make doves appear.
What he did was tie off your friends with a surgical tube,
        piece of lurid chitterling
smudged with grease along its length. Then needle, spoon—
        he did the whole bit,
it was just like in the movies, only your turn turned you
        chicken (or were you defiant?—)
Somebody's got to drive home and that's what you did
        though you'd never
made it even as far as the driveway's end before your dad
        put his foot over the transmission hump
to forestall some calamity he thought would compromise
        the hedges.
All the way back to Evanston you piloted the Mercury
        like General Montgomery in his tank,
your friends huddled in the back seat, spines coiled,
        arms cradled to their ribs—

as though each held a baby being rocked too furiously
        for any payoff less than panic.
It's the same motion your wife blames on some blown-out
        muscle in her chest
when at the end of making love she pitches violently,
        except instead of saying
something normal like *god* or *jesus* she screams *ow! ow!*
        and afterward,
when you try sorting out her pleasure from her pain,
        she refuses you the difference.
Maybe you wish you took the needle at Sczabo's place—
        what's one more stick
among the many you'll endure, your two friends not such
        a far cry from being women,
machines shaking and arching in the wide back seat
        as Sczabo's doves appeared—
or so you thought then, though now you understand
        all the gestures the body will employ
just to keep from puking. Snow was damping the concrete
        and icing the trees,
a silence stoppered in the back of your friends' throats
        as you let the Mercury wheel pass
hand over hand, steering into the fishtails, remembering
        your dad's admonition:
when everything goes to hell the worst you can do
        is hit the brakes.

Cairn for Future Travel

I was young for a minute, but then I got old.
Already the black cane stands by
the threshold, already my feet are flowerpots
in thick black shoes. So not long now
before I will have what follows:

a spidery hairnet to circle my scalp, a hand
callused enough to whack your ear. And with them,
the deep wisdom of Sicilian great-aunts:
how to plumb for the melon's ripeness, how
to stand the loaves upright in my twine sack.

And you, are you ready? Have you brushed
your brown suitcoat and hat? Have you counted
your mahogany chessmen and oiled the zipper
on their leather case? Have you filled
your sack of crumbs for the pigeons?

In the park, men are waiting, raking
the bocce court sand. And as for this second-floor
window where I shake my fist: soon you will learn
to feign deafness, fishing the silver ball
up from your loose, deep pocket.

The Body Rising

*I'd like to do something that would be the opposite of
skydiving. Instead of falling I would rise up and up . . . I
guess I'm talking about flying . . .*

—LETTER FROM VIVIAN KENDALL

Think about the girl in her red bikini,
how she rides the air behind the speedboat.
So what if her chest is leashed to a kite—
forget the kite. Think of county-fair daredevils
careering in rickety turrets, their motorbikes
riding the wall at centrifugal speeds. So what
if you paid a dollar admission—forget the dollar,
forget whatever you admitted. Think of all the times
you didn't have to pay to see gravity break:
the circus clown cannonballed into the sky
and Eva Braun zeppelined into the sky
and the astronauts, especially the astronauts
who never came down when they were turned to vapor.
How to find fault in anything that includes the body rising:
the raft spilling its paddlers, who disappear
so theatrically before they surface in the river's twisted
sheets; the WWII bomber that crashes into the mountain
and stays buried, whose airmen keep floating up
after years in the glacier, limb by perfect limb;

the pillar of smoke rising from the funeral home
run by your neighbors, the monosyllabic
Mills & Burns. For months you've been typing
in a second-story room across the street, oblivious
to what the stories mean—the fact you sit on nothing
more than air, you inhabit the air
just over the oldest bank vault in town, all day
you steep in the waft of silver dollars.
Yet it's not the floor that's important,
not the raft of flowered carpet you think holds everything
up; it's not the kite but the body, not the river
but the body, not the rocket but the body that understands
its elements so well it can revert to them in a blink.
And maybe we serve the body most faithfully
when we abandon it, the way these dancers
(who enter now by way of the TV's local access channel)
allow themselves to rise up on each other's wings.
But these aren't dancers really: they don't have wings.
Just deathmetal punks, speedslammers and moshers
whose choreography's zoned against unbruised escape.
The bass is a wooden shoe clogging
the deepest canal in your ear, and teenage boys
have started to launch themselves like supermans
soaring over the crowd of burnished heads.
You're thinking about what odds these boys risk
getting crushed. But look what happens next:
they don't get crushed. Instead they turn
weightless and waterlogged, bullied and buoyed
like ghosts who can't drown because they have no boats.
Vaults of pliant and complete surrender, rising
as each body passes through the pairs of upraised hands.

Part Three

❧

New Poems

Beige Trash

Who is to blame for there being no tractors
churning the soil into veils
to drape over the telling
where and how I grew, in a suburb
with no men that I could in good conscience adorn
with prosthetic limbs or even crushed straw hats?
Kudzu was something we shouted
jujitsuing air like the Green Hornet's sidekick

whose name still needed some time to ferment
in those years separating the yellow peril
from kung-fu mania, before BRUCE LEE
floated up to the marquee lights.
Like the stripers you could not eat
floating on top of our poisonous river,
to whose bank we never carried our burdens
and let them weep down into Jersey.

Because surely these words would have profited
from at least one silo lording over,
with some earth-moving equipment
parked nearby in a nest of wire
belonging to some good old boy named . . .
what? Leldon? Limuel? But sorry:
in no barn did the whiskey bottles lie
like Confederate casualties at Appomattox—

no tent revivals, no cousins with red hair
and freckled hands, no words as exotic as *po'boy*
or *chifforobe* or *muffaletta*. Which meant
we had no means to wrangle Beauty
into the cathedrals of our mouths,
though on occasion an ordinary cow
could make the car's eight-chambered heart
stop dead beside a pasture, where none of us

dared get out for fear of stampedes or hay fever
or maybe even fangs hidden behind the lips.
Call us ignorant: everything we knew poured out
those two-at-a-time black-and-white TVs—
one for picture, one for sound—& antlered
with coathangers that gave even *Hawaii Five-O*
the speckling of constant winter. The snow
fell like the fur of our fat white dog

for whom my mother cooked lamb chops every night
in an attempt to cure its baldness,
while we dug our fingers in the chopmeat
before she slapped it into patties.
Then *Star Trek* came on. Then for an hour
the men faded in and out of light.
And there is nothing about this past
it does any service to the language to recall:

Art was what the fire department sold tickets to,
raising money for the hook and ladder.
It took place inside the school auditorium,
where an old Italian couple hid
by donning black and standing

just outside the purple spotlight.
Then music surged that was vaguely familiar
though we'd fail to lure its elaborate name

in from the borders of what we knew,
while the marionette-swan bobbled to its feet
as if newly born. I can say it now:
Tchaikovsky. Of course, the whole time
they worked the sticks and strings,
the puppeteers stood right out in the open.
Yet how silently they moved, how easy
a thing they were to pretend we couldn't see.

Foley

It *is* Harrison Ford who just saved the world,
but when he walks down a dirt road toward the ultralarge sun
what sounds like his boots are really bricks being drudged
through a boxful of coffee beans. And the mare you've seen
clopping along those nineteenth-century cobbles—
she's a coconut struck by a ball peen hammer.
And the three girls riding in the hansom,
where the jouncing rustles their silk-and-bone:
that's a toothbrush moving across birchbark.
Even the moment when one kick boxer's perfect body
makes contact with the other kick boxer's perfect body
has nothing to do with kick boxing, or bodies,
but the concrete colliding with the abstract of perfection,
which molts into a leather belt spanking a side of beef.
This is the problem with movies:
go to enough of them and pretty soon the world
starts sounding wrongly synced against itself: e.g.,
last night when I heard a noise below my bedroom window
that sounded like the yowl a cat would make
if its tongue were being yanked backward out its ass.
Pain, I thought. *Help,* I thought,
so at 2:00 A.M. I went outside with a flashlight
and found a she-cat corkscrewed to a tom,
both of them humped and quivering where the beam flattened
against the grass whose damp was already wicking

through my slippers. *Aaah . . . love,* I thought,
or some distantly-cousined feline analogue of love,
or the feline analogue of the way love came out of the radio
in certain sixties pop songs that had the singer keening
antonyms: how can something so right feel so wrong,
so good hurt so bad . . . you know what I'm talking about.
And don't you think it's peculiar:
in the first half of the sixties they made the black girl-groups
sing with white accents and in the second half of the sixties
they made the white girl-groups sing with black accents,
which proves that what you hear is always
some strange alchemy of what somebody thinks you'll pay for
and what you expect. Love in particular
it seems to me we've never properly nailed down
so we'll know it when we hear it coming, the way
screaming "Fire!" *means* something to the world.
I remember this guy who made noises against my neck
that sounded like when after much tugging on a jar lid
you stick a can opener under its lip—that little *tsuck.*
At first I thought this must be
one of love's least common dialects, though later
when I found the blue spots all over I realized
it was malicious mischief, it was vandalism, it was damage.
Everybody has a story about the chorus of these
love's faulty hermeneutics: the muffler in retreat
mistaken for the motor coming, the declaration
of loathing construed as the minor reproach;
how "Babe, can I borrow five hundred bucks?"
gets dubbed over "Good-bye, chump"—of course,
of course, and you slap your head but it sounds funny,
not enough sizzle, not enough snap. If only
Berlitz had cracked the translations or we had conventions
like the international code of semaphores,
if only some equivalent of the Captain Nemo decoder ring

had been muscled across the border. As it has
for my friend who does phone sex
because it's a job that lets her keep at her typewriter all day,
tapping out poems. Somehow she can work
both sides of her brain simultaneously, the poem
being what's really going on and the sex being what sounds
like what's going on; the only time she stops typing
is when she pinches her cheek away from her gums,
which is supposed to sound like oral sex
though she says it's less that it really *sounds* like oral sex
than that these men have established a pact, a convention
that permits them to *believe* it sounds like oral sex.
When they know
it's a woman pinching her cheek and not a blow job,
it's a telephone call and not a blow job,
it's a light beam whistling down a fiber, for god's sake,
and not a blow job. Most days I'm amazed
we're not all schizophrenics, hearing voices
that have been edited out of what calls to us
from across the fourth wall. I've heard
that in *To Have and Have Not* Lauren Bacall's singing
comes from the throat of a man; also that Bart Simpson is really
a middle-aged woman; and last week not once but twice
I heard different women wailing
in public parking lots, the full throttle
of unrestrained grief, and both times I looked straight at them
and pretended nothing unusual was going on,
as though what I was hearing were only the sound of air
shrieking through the spoiler on someone's Camaro.
That's also part of the pact my friend's talking about,
not to offer condolence, not to take note.
You don't tell the men they're sorry creatures,
you don't ask the women what went wrong.
If you're being mugged or raped or even killed,

you have to scream "Fire!" instead of "Help!"
to get someone to help you. Though soon, if not already,
all the helpers will have caught on
and then you'll have to start screaming something else,
like that you've spotted Bacall or Harrison Ford on the street,
Bart Simpson even—no wait a minute, he's not real,
though I remember a time when even the president talked about him
as if he were human. It's not the sleaziness
of phone sex I bristle at, but rather the way it assists
the world in becoming imprecise
about what is real and what is not, what is a blow job
and what is only my friend jimmying her finger
in her mouth or making a sucky noise
against the back of her hand. Which is oddly exactly
how the professor of the ornithology class I took my junior year
taught us to lure birds in, because birds
would think these were the sounds of other birds.
And in that other life of mine,
when bird-watching was something I did for a living,
I remember packing high into the mountains
before the snow melted, when the trail couldn't be followed,
so mine would be the only soul for miles.
One reason I went up there was because at sundown
when the wind climbed the backs of the mountains
along with the spreading violet light,
you could hear the distinct murmuring that the Indians said
were the collective voices of the dead. And I'd lie there,
just my sleeping bag and pad set down on snow,
and I'd look hard at the sky, as though
the wind were something I could see if I looked hard enough,
listening equally hard to convince myself
about the voices of the dead, though always
I was tugged back from true belief
by the one side of my brain that insisted: *Wind.*

And also I remember
how once at the trailhead a man popped out of his motor home
and pointed a camcorder at me, asking
where I was going, what I was doing—though of course,
alone, I wasn't going to say.
But even as I turned away, I heard
the whirr of the movie being made
and the man making up his own narration: *see this little girl,*
she says she's going to climb a mountain,
and briefly I thought about pulling a Trotsky on him
with my ice axe. But as the New Agers say I
"let it go," and I left,
and he didn't follow me, and nothing bad ever happened,
though from time to time I think about strangers watching that movie
in the man's living room, his voice overdubbing
(*see this little girl, she says she's going to climb a mountain*)
the sound of me, of my boots walking.

Trees

I

In late October, daylight stood with one leg in the dark.
A boy swung himself through his unzipped jacket
and worked his feet up. Then monkey-handed he headed
for a part of the branch to be heavier than
and bobbed there like a hunk of suet.
But with girls it was different: you came to a place
where the weight of your fear equaled
the pull of going up, and that was where you stayed.
Your crotch was the anchor you sunk
hard on a limb, and it was enough
to stay hidden in a bonnet of dead leaves
until your mother called your name:
once, twice, her vowelings broke into two notes
that came to you as from whole continents away

II

and I never craved any more perilous instincts,
though sometimes their lack too called out:
the plaster of paris like a missing white fur muff
& my mother never fearful of me falling.
The way I saw her that day my brother shinnied
up our one tall-enough-to-kill-you tree.
The yard sloped from the window above the kitchen sink,

so she could see only where the top of the trunk
tapered, leafless, to a spine that ran
the long axis of his body. I remember
how glamorously—absently, breathlessly—
her hand touched the divot in her neck
as, like a compass needle gauged against the mullion,
he tilted, righted, then slowly tipped the other way.

Air Guitar

The women in my family were full of still water;
they churned out piecework as quietly as glands.
Plopped in America with only the wrong words
hobbling their tongues, they liked one thing
about the sweatshop, the glove factory,
and it was this: you didn't have to say much.
All you had to do was stitch the leather fingers
until you came up with a hand; the rest
they kept tucked to their ribs like a secret book.
Why, was not said, though it doesn't seem natural
the way these women ripped the pages out
and chewed them silently and swallowed—where
is the ur-mother holding court beside her soup pot,
where is Scheherazade and the rest of those Persians
who wove their tragedies in rugs?
Once I tutored a Cambodian girl: each week
I rolled the language like a newspaper and used it
to club her on the head. In return she spoke
a mangled English that made all her stories sad,
about how she'd been chased through the jungle
by ruthless henchmen of Pol Pot; for months
she and her sisters mother grandmothers aunts
lived in the crowns of trees and ate what grew there
and did not touch down. When she told the story,
the way her beautiful and elaborately painted face

would loosen at each corner of her eyes and mouth
reminded me of a galosh too big for its shoe.
It was rubbery, her face, like the words
that sometimes haunt me with their absence,
when I wake up gargling the ghost of one
stuck like a wild hair far back in my mouth.
This morning it took me til noon to fish out
cathexis, and even then I did not know
what this meant until I looked it up.
As it was not until I met her sister
that I learned what the girl was telling me
was not the story she was telling: there were
no women in trees, no myrmidons of Comrade Pot,
their father was, is, had always been,
a greengrocer in Texas. Cathexis:
fixing emotional energy on some object
or idea—say the jungle, or the guy
getting rubbery with a guitar that isn't there.
Yet see how he can't keep from naming
the gut that spills above his belt *Lucille*—
as music starts to pour from his belly
and the one hiked-up corner of his lip. This
is part of a legend we tell ourselves about the tribe,
that men are stuffed and full to bursting
with their quiet, that this is why they've had to go
into the wilderness, searching for visions
that would deliver up their names. While women
stayed in the villages, with language at their center
like a totem log tipped lengthwise to the ground.
And they chipped at it and picked at it,
making a hole big enough to climb in, a dugout
in which they all paddled off to hunt up
other villages, the other members of the tribe.
And when the men returned they found no one home,

just cold fire pits that would not speak—an old
old forsakenness they bring to the bar stools
while the jukebox music washes over each of them
like a tricolored light wheel on a silver tree.
Though someone might argue that none of whatever
I've just said is true: it was men who made boats
while the women sat clumped in private guilds,
weaving their baskets tight enough to trap
the molecules of water. You can see
that the trail from here to the glove factory
would not be terribly long or hard to read,
and how it might eventually lead to the railroad flat
where, alone at night for many years, my grandmother
works deep into her privacy with a common nail
that she scratches across the backs of copper sheets.
She is making either the hands clasped in prayer
or the three-quarter profile of Jesus.
As far as I know there is nothing
the radio can play now that will make her sing.

Self~Portrait in Two Ages

Who is this girl, standing close to the roadway,
flinching in the hard-boiling wake of these trucks?
Okay, it's me—but let's not get nostalgic,
not make this another carousel in Themepark Gone.
Because this girl doesn't want to be me, doesn't want
to be anyone. Even now I can't make her
take on the ghostware of that first-person past.
What she wants is to ride like a Jonah in strange cars
—east, west, it doesn't matter. She wants
the same river again and again and not stepped in
twice. I know: Heraclitus. But don't expect me
to tell her what she wants is that old,
when she thinks it's something that she just invented.
And telling would scold her, like calling her *honey*,
like the woman who clucks into a chalk-white cup
when she looks outside and sees the girl there—
thumb out, head down, hair gone under a watch cap.
There: where the highway tilts onto concrete stalks
across from a steamed diner window. Through which
I'm peering as I cluck into my chalk-white cup.
Even from this distance, I'd know anywhere
my own monkey face, and the city,
there in the arcadia of North American French,
where when a man pulls his car from the current of traffic
she'll get in and let his language surge

between them like another river. She's a boat
without oars, without even a name, and the man
steers her into the murky shallows with a word
that might be *peau* (skin) or *peur* (fear) or *peut*—
as in what he could and could not do. When his hand
slides where her jacket buttons leave a space
like a trough between waves, she'll close her eyes
and say nothing. The river changes but the hand
is always the same, the car moving, or stopped,
as when the hand doesn't belong to a stranger.
She can't tell if she likes it. It's just a hand.   ·
And the woman—who watched her get into the car—
memorizes the license plate, then forgets. It's not him,
after all, that the girl's afraid of. But of living
past him, passing into the someday when she—gone
matronly, stern—will have her own self to answer to.

Apollo

Sleeping bags like matrons' stoles around our necks,
      we were otherwise khaki for the woodlot
where we T-minused until the boys would come
      and feel us up. Zippers
slanted every which way on my thrift-store flight suit
      as the night fell doggedly into the leaves
dropped from fishnet branches where a half-moon blared
      like a transistor radio.
And gravity pooled up both blacker and lesser
      beyond the reach of firelight
where finally the teeth of my centermost zipper
      scratched their cold across my tit.
Only I didn't say tit, think tit, there was no word
      for that landscape
his hand moved across like an exploratory craft,
      like the lunar module after it thrust
away from the ship called *mother* (or *command*)
      and Aldrin and Armstrong disappeared
like children dropping down a shaft. What they named
      for the eagle in fact was a spidery
shape, and imagine history sound-bit that way:
      The Tarantula has landed . . .

Let me skip over the boy, who was a cipher in daylight,
      immaterial, cloudlike:

I could have blown him away. Anyway it was his hand
        not him that stripped the new gears in my chest—
an acetylene sparkage, escorted by noise
        in plurals never heard before on Earth.
The boy had to hiss to shut me up, for making it
        sound like we were *going all the way:*
that's how we talked, in terms of distance,
        as if there came a point from which there were
no turning back. Which turned out to be true,
        though who would have thought
that what we'd go back to is not the time
        before the night, but the night itself
when our synapses sputtered alive like the rocket
        that has waited years inside its shed?
Now I can replicate those same conditions
        —jumpsuit, sleeping bag and hand
probing a landscape that still lacks a name—but the roar
        is never quite so trenchant: sad,
to find the body less attuned to love or will than this
        unmanned, or even chimplike, strangeness . . .

Dugs is a word that comes to mind, like dig, like dirt
        kept in a pail beside the stove;
my breasts are a pair of pajamas guaranteed never to burst
        in unexpected flames.
It's a safety feature: that though the spindle whirs,
        the gears are ground down to their nubs—
a less disconcerting hum of operation, yes,
        but who ever said we'd *want* to be concerted?
I never do the monthly self-exam, forget it;
        at the gym, whenever a chest-scar sails by,
I find myself strangely drawn to its terrain
        as if this were a new moon to explore.

Listen: the old moon, we should have known, was never
      the kind of place anyone could get to twice.
Not and have it be as it was when Aldrin first stood
      cantilevered toward the flag,
an absurd snowman in his absurd suit, while the snow
      peppered our antediluvian TVs.
And would we have paid better attention if we had known
      from that moment on, the moon was through?
If someone had warned us back then that never
      again in our lifetimes would we be so rapt?

The Golden Lotus

My girlfriend's granny had the feet that came
in the film strip after the dowager
empress, before Chiang Kai-shek. To see them,
we would peel her knob-knuckled fingers back
from the felt blanket's stringy satin hem
while she stared out walleyed through the bed rails.
Alone with her, we watched her watching us
afternoons when her daughter went to shop
for the corms and roots the family ate—
which were as knotted as the foot, its toes
a zigzag down the instep. All her life
she had walked on the wrong side of her bones
so girls couldn't run away, my friend said.
And then she'd imitate the tiny steps.

Urged to touch it, I would not, and by June
we drifted, though we assumed twin comas,
making ourselves as dark as nightshade stalks
in neighboring chairs at the public pool.
Where one day she whispered me up a boy
who'd folded her over the staircase rail
when no one was home except for her gran,
who must have heard the bones being levered
into their new shapes. So close I saw her
right there with them, attending them, mumbling

her inconsolable Chinese. And I watched
the old empire rise underneath her shades
when the girl sneered, *It was nothing!*—as if
she'd been affronted by the lack of pain.

Pomegranate

How charitable to call it fruit, when almost nothing
inside it can be eaten. Just the gelatin
that thinly rinds the unpalatable seed.
The rest of it all pith, all bitter,
hardly a meal, even for a thin girl. But food enough,

at least in the myth, to be what ties Persephone
half the year to hell. Thenceforward her name
makes the corn stalks wither: that's why
the Greeks called her *Kore*,
just Kore, meaning *the girl* or *the maid*, the one

who because she was hungry stood no chance against even
the meager pomegranate—though it's never clear
this future isn't the one she wants,
her other choice being daylight, sure,
but also living with her mother. In some versions

she willingly eats the plush red seeds, signing on
with the underground gods and their motorbikes
and their dark shades. Oh . . . all right—
no motorbikes. And *eat*'s not right either.
But what, then—"sucks"? "Strains the seeds against her teeth"?

Of course it would have made more sense for Hades to tempt her
with something full of juice: a grapefruit, say,

or a peach. But maybe these
would be too close to her mother's feast.
And only a girl like Eve could be so blank a slate

to ruin herself with a meal as salutary as the apple.
Give her instead the kind of nourishment
that takes its own hydraulics to extract,
like the pomegranate or the spiny
asteroid of the Chinese chestnut. Or the oyster,

from which, between the riffled shell and shucking knife,
there is no exiting unscathed: a *delicacy,* we say,
whenever the hand hangs out its little
flag of broken skin.
But doesn't the blood that salts the mouth

somehow make the meat taste sweeter? As when she turns
toward us in the moonlight with the red pulp
mottling her teeth: don't our innards
—even if to spite us—start to sing?
I know that's what mine did on those nights

when our girl got called from the junipers
where the rest of us hid her—all it took was his
deep voice, and she stepped out.
Then came sounds that, instead of meaning
carried all of punctuation's weight: the exclamation

when she had her air knocked out, and the question
that was her sudden, inswept breath.
And the parentheses when time went on forever,
when there was no sound because he'd got her by the throat.
He seemed to like our watching, his imperiousness

saying books about how much we didn't know: the jelly

sluiced inside the mouth or the seeds rasped
back and forth across the palate,
until it came time for her to hide behind her own hand
when she had to tongue them out. Sometimes

it would end when the boyfriend strolled her off,
steering as if she were the boat and her skinny arm
were its tiller. But just as often
he'd have somewhere to get to, or lose interest,
as if so much activity had pushed him to the brink of sleep,

and that's how she came back to us kneeling
in our moonlit patch of stunted trees
whose evergreenery wove our hair and pressed
its crewelwork in our haunches. In the half-dark
it would be hard to make out what he'd done: lip pearled,

her chin gleaming like the hemisphere of a tarnished spoon.
But didn't the leaves seem brighter then,
if it can be said that junipers have leaves?
As our hard panting rattled through
. . . but no. Stop here. No of course it can't be said.

Long Time Too Long

A long time, too long, since we have done—this:
abandoned our tools while the sun's still high
and retraced our trail up the attic steps.
The grass still wants mowing as the quilts sigh
back over the bed; the nightshade tendril
winds another turn round the tomato.
But this is work too, this letting clothes fall
in such harsh yellow light that what to do
with what lies underneath them must all be
relearned. Let the vines choke our one good rose,
let the spade stand, the Mason jars empty:
we're sweating enough at each other's lips.
Leave the fallen plums to the white-faced wasps,
beating their drunk wings against the windows.

Crash Course in Semiotics

I

"Naked woman surrounded by police": that's one way
to start the poem. But would she mean anything
devoid of her context, in this case a lushly
late-August deciduous forest, some maple,
mostly oak? She carries no prop—for example,
no bike chain, which the cops could be sawing
from the tree trunk that she's wedded to her body.
But let's start with her pure, and untranslated,
as the famous cartoon of the door is a mystery
until we post the word LADIES at a point that would be
four feet up from the ground if this door
were not drawn two inches tall—it's *us*,
you see, who make believe it corresponds
to a "true-life" human door. Does it help
if I say the naked woman is "really" my true-
life friend, she of the tangled dago surname
we don't need to get into here? And if I say next
that she has been swimming—in Lake Tiorati—

2

you can see how straightaway the tangling subdivides
into a) where the hell is Lake Tiorati?
and b) why naked?—to the last let me answer
that it's 1978 and she is twenty; at college

she's been reading Simone de Beauvoir and learning
words like "patriarchy" and "oppression."
And these have been Mixmastered into her thinking
even about swimsuits—i.e., that not to wear one
is to rip the sign off the door and stomp it
underfoot. When she lies on a rock
the last thing she expects is the tingling
she feels now against her wrist, from a guy
peeing brazenly at her perimeter. This
is an impasse whose bud she thought she had nipped
by aggravating her muscles into interlaced mounds
so her body resembles a relief map of the Appalachians.
In whose northernmost range this story unfolds
& hence the much-delayed answer to item a), above.

3
"Naked woman dadadadada police": not a story but words
at the end of a chain whose first link is her realizing
that the Puerto Rican kids across the lake
splashing and whooping are not having fun—
though this is the sign that she'd stuck on their door.
No, there's another word for the kid
frantically slapping his palms on the water:
Drowning. Even the urinator abruptly stops
his stream and stumbles back from her, ashamed.
And because she's the one with the lifeguard build
and because all the guys are much too drunk,
without even thinking she finds herself paddling
toward the spot these kids are now screaming *Julio!* at,
where she draws a mental *X* upon the water.
Of course, it is a fantasy, the correspondence
that would make a drawing equal life, and so
you understand how amazing it is, when she dives
to the bottom and her hand happens on the child.

4

Perhaps what she expected was for the men on shore
to pay her no mind, as in Manet's *Déjeuner* . . . :
the naked woman sits among them, yet she is a ghost.
But the kids keep yelling *Julio!* even after
she's hauled the wet one out, the one
she points to: *Julio okay.* No, they shriek,
Julio otro! words she knows just enough Spanish
to know means there's another Julio in the lake.
Whom she cannot save despite her next round of diving,
which lasts until the cops come hiking down the trail
in their cop shoes. Then she comes ashore
and stands shivering among them, telling the story
calmly enough until she ends it with: for Christ's sake
can't anyone give her a T-shirt? They're staring
as if somehow she's what's to blame, seeing a naked
woman, not the miracle. Which is, of course,
the living boy, that with these words—*Julio otro!*—
we manage to make sense to anyone at all.

For Edward Hopper,
from the Floor

What I like about the women in Hopper's paintings
is their being given postures anyone could hold—no need
to lie on your side propped up on an elbow,
rotating your head until its gaze is directed
backward athwart your shoulder, a pose
figuring so prominently in the book of nudes
you might be tempted to try it, as I was, on the floor.
And hear a muffled unknuckling, as though the twenty-dollar bills
you've been giving the chiropractor to wad in your spine
have all come unchinked as from old cabin boards,
only it's you there issuing the noise the wind makes
groaning through. The chiropractor: call him Dr. Bruce
to distinguish him from his brothers Drs. Bob and Bill—
at lunch they all go out running together
like a pack of raindrops falling from one cloud.
And just to see them makes my bones ache, the way seeing
the old women who scrubbed tile floors in Mexican hotels
pinged the rubber band stretched in the balsa wood of my chest
because I knew should I get down beside them
within a half-hour my knees would be locked
underrib in perpetuity, like the Land O' Lakes maiden's.

But Hopper will let you just sit there, slumped
in that very unergonomic chair, sobering in light

from a not-too-difficult sun, and you don't have
to be slender. And you don't have to pretend
that the collie dog standing chest-deep in the grass
doesn't secretly irritate you with her virtues.
And Dr. Bruce will not crawl into that space
between the hotel dresser and the narrow hotel bed
to demonstrate stomach crunches or those doggie exercises
supposed to pop your sacral vertebrae back in place.
Or Dr. Bob, Dr. Bill—but for the color of their nylon shoes
they are interchangeable, the way Hopper's women
all share the body of his wife, Jo, whom he drew
often with a crumbly rust-colored crayon
called sanguine, I've learned: after the French for blood.

For I Have Taught the Japanese

whilst sitting with my fanny on the desk,
which is not done in their country
someone who knew later said.
And hectored them in words they did not understand,
though I spoke loudly and clipped each one off
like Don Quixote pruning dead blooms from a rosebush.

And now that they have long since traveled back
into the pebble gardens of their lives, I wonder
if they remember any more of me than the pretzel shapes
my lips squirmed through, the ones that betrayed
my disapproving their enthusiasm for the mall
where they bought accessories silk-screened with obscure

American cartoon characters like Ziggy—& see
how I raise him now against them like a studded club?
For didn't I envy their aptitude at old, masonic arts
like ballroom dance and bowling, my own wild gutter balls
bounding them to the brink of a genuine sadness
they also fastened to my spinsterhood: "No, really,"

I had to tell them, "it's okay." I was such
an idiot I even tried to apologize more than once

for Nagasaki, their reply held back until one night
when they made floating lamps from paper bags and candles.
And watching the orange smudges ride into the deep
blue-black of the lake, at last I understood

that I understood not one thing about grace, whose anatomy
is mostly silent. Toward the end of the term
they took a class picture then would not show me it
for weeks, so I imagined an open button or a scrap
of lettuce blackening my teeth. But I turned out
I thought normal among them, camouflaged in my blue dress,

and have never learned what about me made them
hang their heads over their desks, the hair
falling down over each face like a puppet-show curtain
shut across the moon, until someone reclaimed the photo
as if taking something sharp back from a child
and elocuted very crisply: There now, Lucia-san, you see.

Pigeons

It must have been Lucifer the fallen angel
who dreamed up their trick coats: the purple

green indigo flashing on like thunderclaps
then going dim, whenever a fat cloud blimps

across the sun. On window ledges outside every office
of every stupid job I've ever held, they made me witness

the feathers trapping not just air and light
but other atmospheric fallout too: the clod of shit

dingling around the haunches and the gray leaves
wattled to the breast. Not many groomed themselves;

most acted as if grooming were a vanity
that they'd transcended, mystics, gurus, all belly

trundling on dainty feet that somehow managed to concoct
a swagger. The hen would not

return my gaze when the male began to harry her
until she let him get behind and lumber

up.
Then I'd hear the flywheel of their passion slip:

❦

Hhyungh Hhyungh Hhyungh Hhyungh Hhyungh Hhyungh
... like the roommate I had once

who could not stop the joy at midpoint in her throat
and let it go in sloppy blooms that echoed

through the ducts.
While I waded the sahara of my zoology texts:

Hhyungh Hhyungh Hhyungh ... you can see how much
of life I've spent distracted, how jobs I've botched

now blossom up behind me like the down and dust
their plumage sloughs, clouds of exhaust

that trail behind them on the ledges.
What would a wing be, though, without its feathers

—half a living coat hanger?
And what would a pigeon be then, but a salamander

gorged on too much Spanish fly.
Look in the dictionary

and here's what you get: *Columbidae, family of birds
having deep chests, short legs and smallish heads,*

which reminds me of the Italian girls I knew in high school
and didn't count myself among, though I was one too:

had just the short legs. Negligible chest.
Spent most of my life embarrassed by sex,

shame being what does not lapse of Catholic legacy.
And so I marvel at these pigeons, who will not easily

quit humping, no matter how loud I bang the glass.
What they usually do is pretend they're deaf;

sometimes they'll disengage and waddle a slow Mae West
toward the ledge lip, from which they heave their breasts

and let them fall a ways before they flap—
as if to prove that heaven will always bear them up.

The Sportsmen's Guide

—for my nephew on his birth

In the redneck survivalist catalogue, tucked in
with the Vietnam-issue tomahawks and the camouflage
lingerie, they're hawking a T-shirt: *I entered the world*
fat, mad, and bald, and I plan on leaving that way.
This is the old man I see ghosting your face,
you who have such big hands for an old man.
You were late, and my sister explains how they had to use
what she's calling "the salad tongs" to yank you
out. Can't say that I blame you
for not being eager to join us here, we whose talents
fall equally between the making and the ruining.
So the salad tongs have left a red bruise on your face:
welcome to America. Pretty soon
we'll have to get you a lawyer so you can get cracking
on your due. Or perhaps you'd be interested
in some of this Red Army ammo
that the demand for hard currency has made a steal
at less than a hundred bucks a crate? You'll see:
there are plenty of ways of getting even. Someday
you could even write a poem, the tradition of which
pretty much demands the reader be told off the bat
what a muckheap the world is. But then comes the swerve
where the poet flipflops or digresses
to come up with *something* that the muckheap

will surprise you with. Like on the day you were born
when, here, the full breadth of America away,
the sky was suffering what looked like an exceptional
bloom of weed-fluff. Turned out to be ladybugs
looping on oversized wings, which disappeared
under polka-dotted hulls everywhere they lighted.
Ladybugs that rode my sleeves all day.
So don't listen to me: be glad
the doctors wrenched you from your private swamp.
The bruise will fade, and the world will appear to you in ways
both more beautiful and more terrible than you could ever
imagine, you who weighed in a half-pound heavier
than even Ivan Turgenev's formidable brain.

Serotonin

Let be be finale of seem.
—WALLACE STEVENS

At year's end, the news from here
concerns the new ordinance against couches: no couches
allowed on porches anymore, except for those designed

for outdoor use. The mayor thinks we'll feel better
after the banishment of all that soggy misused foam,
corollary to the gray mood that shall be lifted

like a beached log by the tide. But you know me,
already worrying how to know this outdoor couch
now that a fifty-dollar citation rides on the difference

between velour and vinyl, rattan and wicker,
cushion and mat. Last night was the solstice:
I spent it shivering around a forty-gallon drum whose flame

we party creatures were to feed with slips of paper
inscribed with our woes from this year past.
But I wanted to burn nothing and stood there flummoxed

by my strange absence of regret ... until I remembered
the nightly tablets reminiscent of moths, the white
generics the pharmacist swears are the same

as the yellow pills that January started with.
And I do feel better—though humbled, a bit foolish
to figure such heartsickness a matter of ions

merely orbiting a lobe of brain, much like the hydrangea
at the southeast corner of the house, how it becomes
a blue shrub if you bury old nails in its roots. This

I don't get: how one day the tide marsh at sunrise
can make your blood overrun your chest, and the next day
it's just a sweatshop for salt flies, the rain

a thorn nest on your head. Or how the eagle
detendoning a heron carcass here
where the Skokomish River has outrun its banks

can be, for my friend up in Canada, just one
more emblem of America's mawkishness & glop.
He calls them shithawks, having seen so many

galumphing bedraggled through the dump, where they slit
the mountain of shiny sacks in search
of undigested grease. And yet it's the same bird

that made me drive into a fence post
while I gawked at the deluged field—amazed, amazed
I ever wanted not to be here. News flash:

what's been walking around in my clothes all these years
turns out to have been a swap meet of carbons
and salts: what can be poured into the ground to make

the hydrangea red again. As the sadness inherent
in a wet clime's winter might just be this same
image thing, a moldy beach ball smell that'll disappear

once we straighten out the business with the couches.
Meanwhile someone tell Wallace Stevens he was wrong about seem:
Seem is good. Seem is everything.

Lament in Good Weather

So would this be how I'd remember my hands
(given the future's collapsing trellis):
pulling a weed (of all possible gestures),
trespassing the shade between toppled stalks?
A whole afternoon I spent chopping them back, no fruit
but a glut of yellow buds, the crop choked
this year by its own abundance, the cages
overrun. And me not fond of tomatoes, really,
something about how when you cut to their hearts
what you find is only a wetness and seeds,
wetness and seeds, wetness and seeds.
Still, my hands came gloved with their odor
into this room, where for days I've searched
but found no words to fit.
Bitter musky acrid stale—the scent
of hands once buried past the wrist in vines.

Brief Life Among
the Immortals

Years ago we met the famous woman
the day my cousin was to marry a son of the son
she'd propagated from the mulch of her most famous
unhappy love. Long before it was the fashion,
she'd cropped her long hair at the ears, had laid
her long bones down on the analyst's brocaded couch
and written one long book whose purpose, it seemed,
was our deliberate bewilderment. Such words
she made leap inside our mouths—*socialist*
and *suffrage*. But we never spoke them, *free love*
being the kind of trout whose wild jewelry
would fade as soon as we plucked it from the river.

She was also old by the time we met, with an orchid
pinned to her collar and skin as powdery as starch.
I remember being launched toward the shoals of her
like a longboat sent to spear the whale:
I believe she may have even deigned to stoop
before she petted me. Then the adults followed,
jury-rigging the bloodline into their rope bridge
across which they how-do-you-doed on nervous tiptoe.

For this purpose, my mother had bought me a new dress
shocking in its chic, an iridescence of layers

the color of rain. My cousin wore a sixties mini
instead of the regulation pouf, in retrospect a portent
for the way her marriage too fell short—
the grandson ran off, the famous woman died.
And in bitterness we were restored too quickly
to that unadorned first-person-plural past. From which
her face swims in a magazine today, holding me
once again in its regard. Then I am satin
glowing in the reprised old stone church
where we wait for her taxi, as shy as brides.

Palimpsest

Right now, somebody is logging his name in the shore.
With his big toe. Or with a driftstick.
Or with a broken bottle tumbled milky by the surf.
Every day someone declares himself
and every day the sea comes up and wipes him out;

could be a name, could be love's barbwire barb
that's a plus sign cartwheeling between capital letters.
Or could be something you'd think capable of putting up
a bigger fight: say a car that has run off the hardpan
and sunk to its axles on a rising tide—as in: gee,

they drove down the beach to kiss in the moonlight
and now their not-even-paid-for sport utility vehicle
is nosing off in the general direction
of the Mariana Trench. Never mind that in college
we learned whatever number thermodynamic law it was

that says matter can neither be destroyed nor created:
it only goes elsewhere. *Elsewhere,*
like those seven thousand plastic ducks
shucked loose when their cargo ship broke up at sea.
Or like the seven thousand books I must have read

that have floated across the curved horizon of my brain,
so that now Pythagoras is just a trench coat in the shadows

and Socrates is elsewhere with his cup of leaves
and Plato is gone, and Hegel is gone,
and Jacques Derrida is a Winnebago trundling the deeps . . .

This I commit to memory forever: the command
I closed my eyes and forced myself to swallow like a hook
after reading certain passages by Virginia Woolf
or watching elk lap off the bog at dusk. And still
the breakers of elsewhere rose up and wiped me

like a vigorous waitress with her spray,
until both Woolf and elk were gray and gone
and in their absence more or less the same.
Yet he made it look so easy, the biology professor,
who told the two hundred assembled freshmen us

that in twenty years all we'd remember from his class
was this: that men with Klinefelter's syndrome
have testicles the size of peas. And it worked,
though now I marvel why it did, when the fact
is empty baggage. And why does my childhood dream

of fire hats floating out a culvert pipe in my hometown
stick? But not Plato, who has floundered off
in cloudy collegiate bongwater toward my brain's
furthest neural atoll, where he lies hidden
under the cucumber slices he's got covering

his eyelids? Oh, he knows about the sun
lathering the cocoa butter on his thighs, but not
how they're also being embossed by the lounge chair's
quasi-raffia-textured webbing, a memory on the verge
of being obsolesced by plastic, by that ass-

supporting ligature that sags but will not snap
and resists water-rot just like those seven thousand ducks.
Someday—between the year 2000 and 2013—
one of them is already predicted to ebb toward a beach
where a teenager in army fatigues might nudge it

with his Kalashnikov and say *"pato"*: Tagalog for duck.
Which will matter only if he reports back
to the scientists in Seattle; otherwise, it'll be
just one more fleeting detail this world supplies
so many of that you might ask why even bother

bringing the matter up? In my dream, the fire hats
could also float back into the culvert and disappear
upstream. And here's something about Pythagoras
I do remember: that before they rolled their bedding
he made his students wipe the impress of their bodies out.

A Readymade

Our of nowhere the phone rings, and the voice
of a fat man answers: Hell-low bay-bee . . .
each syllable its own word. "Chantilly Lace":
a song not sung so much as fumbled through,
a manifesto of befuddlement and pleasure—*call it*
a little game between "I" and "me" said Marcel Duchamp
when asked why he'd hang a porcelain urinal
in the Grand Central exhibition, where people
would be expecting to see . . . well, something else.
Something not a urinal. It is a matter of record
the fat man's name was J. P. Richardson, a.k.a.
The Big Bopper, whose purchase on history boils down
to these questions: *Do I what?* and *Will I what?*
Plus the fact of his going down in the plane
that also killed Ritchie Valens and Buddy Holly
the night my head was battering the gates
of my mother's cervix—when the phone rang for me,
by God I was going to answer (hello baby).
The problem is usually not so much what to include
as what to leave out: you can see how the urinal
establishes a precedent for putting any
old thing up there on the wall—a snow shovel,
a bicycle seat, a "Do I what?" a "Will I what?"
Pretty soon all you'd want to do is play chess
as a way of narrowing the field—*I am only*

a breather Duchamp said later, and the urinal
got thrown away by someone who mistook it for trash.
Some distinctions elude us, such as whether
the Beechcraft did or did not disappear
in a preternaturally glowing cloud, the night
the world asked *Will I what?* and I said
Yes. Shucked off my animal-skin coat
and left it scattered among the wreckage
the day the music died, in an otherwise empty field.

Abandon

Only alone can I really dance now.
And only in the large rooms of an empty house.
When night throws me back in from the windows

in these more auburn and elastic versions
wavering across the glass. The songs
do what songs do—hoist the dumbbells of their refrains—

the backup girls go *chain chain chain:* one thing
undamaged by the shopwear of the present's
sliding back into the past, that past

whose windows were always hidden
behind blinds made from southeast-Asian weeds.
And the philodendron wobbled rhythmically to the din

as if it were sentient, in those houses
where everyone was but nobody lived
except for this guy named Gypsy due back any minute

with two kilos of Hawaiian dope and some
washed-out washed-up Ann-Margret usedtabe in tow.
Meanwhile each night bled into the next, like stories

told to hold the knife off someone's throat,
the scratches on the record pattering
like pine needles dropping to the forest floor

as the music rained in shiny dollops
that I took for either Liquid Nail gluing us together
or Liquid Plumber eating away our skin, either way

it was a case of the many being forged
into the one, like wax dribbled from many candles
become a cuneiform blob atop the empty bottle of Matteus

that was kept as an erotic totem beside the bed.
Nights of that same particolored
and striated dripping down: in the morning

sometimes there'd be so much broken furniture
you just threw it out and started new
with a different Dumpster sofa, a chain

of mildewed plaids I remember coming to an end
around the time of vinyl's being vanquished
by the compact disc. It happened

during a communal meltdown to the Talking Heads,
when the famous someone's wayward daughter
got juiced on too much melon cordial

and tore a big gash in the noise's silk, dragging
the needle across the radius of the whole LP
in one terrifying zip. Everyone stood there, swaying

a bit like underwater reeds while she sleuthed out
Janis Joplin's Greatest Hits and commenced screeching
like a war widow who's just learned the news about her dead.

How precarious the glue of our communion.
If you have watched schooling fish, you know
how goes this surrendering to shimmer: their brains

are nothing, yet each one thinks its pronoun's making
something larger of itself as seen from outside
the iridescent clump. But let one grow weak

and the rest will chew its eyeballs out, as the drunk
can slip over fellowship's Niagara Falls
in the space of a swallow. Later that night

a rocking chair would catch on fire
and be carted outside to a snowdrift, where it
would take on hypnotic, quasireligious qualities . . .

but this was before the ember fell into the cushion
and smoldered there while the wallboard throbbed;
this is the woman singing and the shrill spume made

from a ground-up piece of her heart spurting
like bitter sludge from a syringe's tip.
And this is also me going down to the basement

where the rags that once were panties stiffen
and clot together in the inky dark, where I'm batting
my arms until one intersects the light-switch string

and there comes an almost audible hosanna
from the circuit box that'll shut her up.
With the floorboards groaning overhead, I open it

and pop the breakers like a backbone, tango-dipped.
Then silence swallows us in its black gullet.
Next comes the rocker's bursting into flames.

Tilapia

One day a man just walks out on his life:
for two months and two weeks and two days now
he's missing. The newspaper tells us
not to put too much faith in his beard
—the beard could have been scrapped in any city.
Or his clothes—by now the plaids are worn
to a geometry of threads. If we are to know him
we will know him by his word, *tilapia*:

the fish he planned to farm someday.
African cichlid. Food of the future.
Tilapia: even if he's got amnesia
his wife is sure this word would stick.
And it must be amnesia—why else
would he be spotted on a train crossing Montana
with the geranium of a wadded tissue pressed
to his brow? *Tilapia*: what we walk out on,

what we take with us, what we use as flint
to see what sparks when everything goes black.
Amnesia, or not: someone else reports him
shooting craps in Vegas, blowing hot air
on his dice, and if his head looked bloody
it was from a taller woman's kiss. *Tilapia*:
the fish scale's flash, the good-bye to everything
that doesn't glitter. When I was a kid

the game I liked best was simply spinning,
letting the world smear into one big blur
until the me did not exist and everything
was me, the wavering grass and the zigzag sun.
I didn't care for the way it ended though,
the way you fell down and gave yourself a name—
leopard, teapot, three-legged stool. You could not
stay nothing. And the form of the game

traced the arc of a life: first you drifted
then you settled. Okay to float for a while
on the highway's velvety exhaust, wearing a poncho
and the incognito of rain—so long
as these years lead back to the mailbox
with its red flag to remind you when you're home.
Tilapia: the keys in the pocket, the unloosenable
knot. I'm alarmed, for example, when sometimes

I can't remember my husband's name. And likewise
I am troubled by his lack of scent. He smells
like tapwater, which does not travel
in the valise of my skin, or bind like a rope
so that I could run only to the hard end
of its length. Running: another skill
I practiced as a kid, not the scissoring legwork
but the idea of escape. Hours spent

under the porch where latticework doled out
the daylight. Hours spent making a hole so deep
it would open on the other side of Earth.
I pictured words falling from my mouth
like all the junk in my pockets as I walked

upside down in China. *Tilapia:*
bookmark to an open book, its pages blank
but faintly rumpled, as though from the moisture

of flowers that had been pressed there once.
Tilapia: my husband in those spaces where
he has no name but is not missing. *Tilapia:*
that someone glimpses the man on a park bench
in Fresno, where his wound is cherry filling
from a TableTalk pie. *Tilapia:* the way my mother
would step out on the porch and call my name
and I'd come back, just because she was so pretty.

In Light of the Absent Constant

I don't trust the few fixed sums, like the speed
of the light that falls precisely on the lawn,
there, but not *there*, clap on, clap off—
to indicate the shadow of the tree.
Something suspicious about that kind of precision
coming from something moving as fast as
the speed of light: you would think
we'd be dealing with a blurry edge. Blur I could trust
in what comes from a distance: the static,
the garble, the disconnect. But too clear
is your voice from this bone-shaped white thing
that looks as if it belongs in the nose of a giant pygmy.
And always I'm either talking on the phone or else
I'm switched off: the automaton me, the binary me, the me
who's a string of zeroes behind the wheel.
Like Mr. Magoo, who offends me not
for his depiction of the visually disabled
but more because when the rest of us happen to drive
off the metaphorical drawbridge, how come
the barge never happens to be passing underneath?
I mean, haven't we simplified a bit here?
Told little white lies, to put someone's mind at ease?
Though some say the world will boil down
to one equation, once we get the physics squared away,
one number like Avogadro's 6.023

times 10^{23}, having to do with molecules and moles.
Though say the word "mole"
and no doubt most people will think of a creature
burrowing through the dirt, with hands
like old leather gloves crushed up
against its cheeks. What scares me is not
just the fracture hazard posed by the holes in the lawn,
but more this idea that we don't even know what's going on
under our own feet. Come back soon,
I am troubled. I'm like that woman whose voice
inhabits the machines: *if you'd like to make a call*
please hang up and dial again . . . & not so much that part
as the *bwoop bwoop bwoop bwoop.* It's hard to maneuver
with so much dirt raining down—I am a mole
whose number is fixed at minus one.
Minus one minus one minus one minus one.
Then the phone rings, and I blunder back to light.

The Sutro Baths

They were the viscera inside the city,
another window in a row of windows painted black,
a name trafficked in the freebie papers, hothouse

orchid without any petals, the sex parts gorged
& become the flowering's lusher hub. The Sutro Baths
were supposed to be, I guess you'd say, "co-ed": sometimes

I thought of tooling there in my Toyota,
diagonally parking nearby in that grease-dark,
wearing I can't imagine what under my coat; there are limits

past which these pictures will not take me, shielding
my face from the recording angels, Garbo-like
as I shadow my shadow in. Here's what I think

the bland door conceals: a maze of chambers
gilded with the tapestries of random touch
and everywhere the gothic battlements of muscles bullied

into torsion's strenuous relief. And the walls
wear us but golden, multiplied and misconstrued
by mirrors capable of distorting paunches into flames

and interlocked like paisley, knobs nesting into bays.
Where I could be a man with buttocks cut from marble
or a bald girl with no flap or fold of her unhooped

—denizen, maenad, fury, Fate.
And out of these clichés the wet steam rises
but no water, save what runs too loudly in my head:

slosh of my heart's valves and chambers
amplified, private, like the sea inside a shell.
I'm talking early eighties, before the virus,

wrong—: after the virus but before the virus had a name;
it seemed there was less need for putting words to things,
the 1-900 number and the hotline, no call

even for lettering the plywood marquee—somehow
we would just know which door to enter.
But there is no entering the Sutro Baths, suspended

as they are inside the brain's hermetic seal, no going there
with the carpetbag of a real belly: so did I chicken
out by going east to school instead? Where all we did

was try to build that place in daylight
using the endless mirrors of our talk—
say about Foucault, the bathhouse specter, by the end

a wading bird in his kimono. And George Bataille, who wrote
of the body "reeling blindly towards annihilation,"
and of how the ancient Dionysian rites

were meant to spark a lust-contagion in the crops
—as though the corn could read this alphabet
of naked limbs and would then frenzy up with silk

(and say the word, or think it: *tassel*). We saw slides
from the Villa of Mysteries, frescoes of women
bearing the statue of the giant penis; they taught us to speak

these cryptograms—*lingam, priapic*—anything
could be uttered once it had a code, a terminology
either obscurely latinate, or French: *jouissance,*

plaisir, all the bite hung up in back the throat
so that what talk emerged had its murk filtered.
Outside the brain's bright package, the baths are nothing

but one nugget of obsidian,
impenetrable *and* fathomless, like the crystal globe
or tea leaves or the viscera inside of which

the gypsy claims she can see pictures. In bas-reliefs
exhumed from the Villa of Mysteries, the woman
spreads her legs like antlers lacing overhead;

the man curls from her in an unnatural display.
And though their coupling decorates an ordinary cup, there is
no bridge between it and our living, we

whose bodies reside here in the prison of
their common, human poses. This desire is no language
we could articulate, or execute—say *execute*—

but that the words are hollow doesn't mean they come
without their dangers. In school, reading too many
left me half-blind, my eyes in need of, as we say,

correction. Have not been back to San Francisco
since I left, though I've heard
the bathhouse scene is past. Often I wonder

what crops were there to grow from that contagion—
the window box, the city garden? Or oysters, maybe
something that thrives on what the waters smash and scatter.

In the Long Shadow of
Pierre de Fermat

In his poem it's not yet daylight
and the young man's mom is headed south,

when suddenly out of the dawn-broth a horse
appears in the road too close for braking.

But don't panic, she's all right; he says
for once she happens to be wearing her seat belt,

and it's a soft horse, or a strong fender,
an air bag, angel, just dumb luck—a miracle

being no more than a fraction, the one
out of god-knows-what that the young man,

my student, is driving at in his poem:
the ratio with its own double dot of deliverance

that's got the whole class dreamily veering off,
remembering what it was like to dive

from the highest point in the quarry rim
and come down so close to a granite sleeper

just below the water's duckweed skin
that they rasped the tips of their perfect noses

and took the inch that spared their skulls for proof
of the apportionment of grace. Oh, and it breaks

my heart to have to be the one who tells them
that for every soft horse there will come

a dozen harder down the pike, and who'll
be cowering behind the wheel when they appear

but one of us—*out of us!*—who never
planned on being the numerator

but only part of that large denominator
standing for the whole generic mush.

The Oldest Map

with the Name

America

I
In Martin Waldseemüller's woodblock, circa 1507,
the New World is not all there.
We are a coastline
without substance, a thin strip
like a movie set of a frontier town.
So the land is wrong and it is empty,
but for one small black bird facing west,
the whole continent outlined with a hard black edge
too strictly geometric, every convolution squared.
In the margin, in a beret, Amerigo Vespucci
pulls apart the sharp legs of his compass—
though it should be noted that instead of a circle
in the Oldest Map with the Name America
the world approximates that shape we call a heart.

2

The known world once stretched from my house
to the scrim of trees at the street's dead end,
back when the streets dead-ended instead of cleaving
into labyrinths of other streets. I was not
one of those who'd go sailing blithely
past the neighborhood's bright rim:
Saturdays I spent down in the basement
with my Thingmaker and Plastigoop . . .
Sunday was church, the rest was school,
this was a life, it was enough. Then one day
a weird kid from down the block pushed back
the sidewall of that edge, spooling me
like a fish on the line of his backward walking
fifty yards deep into the woodlot. Which
was barely wild, its trees bearing names
like sugar maple, its snakes being only
garter snakes. Soon the trail funneled
to a single log spanning some unremarkable
dry creek that the kid got on top of,
pointed at and said: You fall down there,
you fall forever. And his saying this
worked a peculiar magic over me: suddenly
the world lay flat and without measure.
So that when I looked down at the dead leaves
covering the ravine they might have
just as well been paint, as depth
became the living juice squeezed out
of space: how far
could you fall? Then the leaves shifted,
their missing third dimension reconfigured
into sound: a murmuring snap
like the breakage of tiny bones that sent me
running back to the world I knew.

3

Unlike other cartographers of his day,
Waldseemüller wasn't given to ornamenting his maps
with any of Pliny's pseudohuman freaks,
like the race of men having one big foot
that also functions as a parasol.
Most likely he felt such illustrations
would have demeaned the science of his art,
being unverifiable, like the rumored continents
Australia, Antarctica, which he judiciously leaves out.
Thus graced by its absence, the unknown world
floats beyond the reach of being named,
and the cannibals there
don't have to find out yet they're cannibals:
they can just think they're having lunch.

4

My point is, he could have been any of us:
with discount jeans and a haircut made
by clippers that his mother ordered
from an ad in a women's magazine.
Nothing odd about him except for maybe
how tumultuously the engines that would run
his adult body started up, expressing
their juice in weals that blistered
his jaw's skin as its new bristles
began telescoping out. Stunned
by the warped ukelele that yesterday had been
his predictable voice, the kid
one day on the short-cut home from practice
with the junior varsity wrestling squad
came upon a little girl in the woods
where what he did was nameless & terrible
& ended with something written on her stomach.
Bic pen, blonde girl: the details ran
through us like fire, with a gap
like the eye of the flame where you could
stick your finger and not get burnt.
By sundown the whole family slipped,
and the kid's yellow house hulked
empty and dark, with a real estate sign
canted foolishly in its front yard.
Then for weeks our parents went round
making the noise of baby cats
stuck up in trees: who knew? who knew?
We thought they were asking each other
what the kid wrote with the Bic——
what word, what map——and of course
once they learned the answer
they weren't going to say.

5

In 1516, Martin Waldseemüller
draws another map in which the King of Portugal
rides saddled on a terrifying fish.
Also, the name "America"
has been replaced by "Terra Cannibalor,"
with the black bird changed to a little scene
of human limbs dangling from trees
as if they had been put up there by shrikes.
Instead of a skinny strip, we're now
a continent so large we have no back edge,
no westward coast—you could walk left
and wind up off the map. As the weird kid did—
though the world being round, I always half-expect
someday to intersect the final leg of his return.

6

Here the story rides over its natural edge
with one last ornament to enter in the margin
of its telling. That is, the toolshed
that stood behind the yellow house,
an ordinary house that was cursed
forever by its being fled. On the shed
a padlock bulged like a diamond,
its combination gone with all the other
scrambled numbers in the weird kid's head,
so that finally a policeman had to come
and very theatrically kick the door in
after parking one of our town's two squad cars
with its beacon spinning at the curb.
He took his time to allow us to gather
like witnesses at a pharaoh's tomb,
eager to reconstitute a life
from the relics of its leaving.
And when, on the third kick, the door flopped back
I remember for a moment being blinded
by dust that woofed from the jamb in one
translucent, golden puff. Then
when it settled, amid the garden hose
and rusty tools we saw what-all
he'd hidden there, his cache
of stolen library books. Derelict,
lying long unread in piles that sparked
a second generation of anger . . .
from the public brain, which began to rant
about the public trust. While we
its children balled our fists
around the knot of our betrayal:
no book in the world had an adequate tongue
to name the name of what he did.

7

Dying, Tamburlaine said: Give me a map
then let me see how much is left to conquer.
Most were commissioned by wealthy lords,
the study of maps being often prescribed
as a palliative for melancholy.
In the library of a castle of a prince
named Wolfegg, the two Waldseemüller maps
lay brittling for centuries—"lost,"
the way I think of the weird kid as lost
somewhere in America's back forty, where
he could be floating under many names.
One thing for sure, he would be old now.
And here I am charting him: no doubt
I have got him wrong, but still he will be my conquest.

8

Sometimes when I'm home we'll go by the house
and I'll say to my folks: come on,
after all these years it's safe
just to say what really happened.
But my mother's mouth will thin exactly
as it did back then, and my father
will tug on his earlobe and call the weird kid
one mysterious piece of work.
In the old days, I assumed
they thought they were protecting me
by holding back some crucial,
devastating piece. But I too am grown
and now if they knew what it was
they'd tell me, I should think.

La Vie en Rose

The pine barrens were burning.
And we thought this was maybe how the world would end:
thin smoke getting thicker. Closing in
on the nuclear power plant near Manahawkin.

Ours must have been one of the last cars they let through,
headed south, not about to turn back. Imagine—
the Jersey Turnpike a beeline to oblivion!
The idea made my father silence the radio
with one of his arm's jaunty sweeps
whose backhand launched an Edith Piaf tape,
her voice like little men running up and down on sand.
He sang along in a bricklayer's tenor: ya-da-dee . . .
when the notes went high he geared them down into his throat.

He didn't understand a word, though. Sometimes
he swatted my mother's knee: what's she saying?
"Always love," my mother answered. Or, "I lived for love."
Until finally he gets it—*amour!* love! the end of the world!

Somewhere flames hopped toward a cyclone fence,
levers were thrown, a red circle drawn
on a map. Yet I don't think we were ever more happy—
my father singing, the road furrowing the braided limbs.

Home

In Renaissance paintings, it's somewhere apart
from the peopled scene. A somewhere whose trees
grow in spires or in cordial tufts, and each rock
is deliberate, a fragment of the chipped world

washed, tumbled, reset. At least that's what we see
through the window in Ghirlandaio's painting
of the grandfather with his famously warted nose:
the trees and the river horseshoeing toward

the purplish, symmetric butte. A pastoral elsewhere.
Someplace to offset this man and his blebs
buckling one on the next. When we know what's really
outside the window—Florence's open sewers,

beggar-child X and Signor Y's ulcered foot—
after all, this is the fifteenth century, every rat
packing off its plague-fleas to the next new town.
No wonder Ghirlandaio puts that town someplace

the rats could never get to from here, not without
scaling a glacier or paddling through water
whose purity would be the weir that strains them out.
Even Saint Sebastian, in frescoes by Mantegna

and Pollaiuolo, becomes foreground to a river
that runs from mountains jacketed in snow.
But lacking shadow, depth . . . as if to ask us
what good perspective is in dire circumstances,

like here, now, Saint Sebastian with an arrow sticking
through his head. Ghirlandaio, Pollaiuolo—
it took a trip to the library to rekindle the names,
and on my way home to write them down, I stopped

to buy some bread at Bayview Grocery. It's a place
that reminds me of those paintings: something
about how the dust congeals into a yellow varnish
gilding the labels on the cling-peach tins,

but here, outside, the Sound also plunges a foamy arm inland
beside the Dumpster. And if you stand at the parking lot's
western edge on cloudless days, you see tall peaks
tinted by distance, with nothing else in the landscape

to match their shades—the purples and salmony orange
and full-blown, flamingo pink almost too
too lavish, as though whatever god made them were running
for a city council seat. Of course

when you get there, the mountains are never purple,
and come evening the mist slides down the couloirs
to settle in the back crease of your neck. But from here
doesn't *there* look romantic, aren't you shanghaied

by its Shangri-la, and don't you start thinking
about the Kennedy administration, doesn't it make you feel
like being kissed? Nearby the city council's commissioned
a concrete man and woman to do just that: kiss

til kingdom come while her knee rises underneath
her dress. It's a civic-minded embrace, though: one woman
and one man oblivious to her breasts, quite different
from what's going on by the pay phone, where one man

grapples with another. Not lovers, their bodies big
with the scent of dead leaves turned. The heavier man
leans back against the ice freezer while the smaller man
kneels before him like a supplicant, their drunkenness

a lifeboat swamped by words. And I hear something
about five dollars missing, which makes the bigger man
take down his pants—to prove what he has, which is nothing
but the lumpy glands pooled in his hand, a gesture

whose earnestness in another context might seem almost
touching. But the friend is touching, isn't touched,
bug-eyed with scrutiny and stern outrage as he pokes
through what is offered like a nest of pale blue eggs

—though *friend* is probably too strong a word
to link these men who only happen to be trapped together
when a pie-piece of the world shears off: my slice
between parking spot and doorway in. Already a woman

is directing traffic away while I stop to look.
My guess is that these guys come from the lean-tos
of corrugated metal scavenged along the chop,
about which there are letters in the paper every day

that go: *How come these lowlifes get to live by the inlet
while the rest of us have to shell out every month*

for crummy solid walls? And they're made out of what—
Sheetrock? Cardboard pancaked with chalk? Ten years ago

I'd have said people live by the inlet because
the human creature, even in its trials, seeks beauty out.
But now I think that come nightfall the beautiful place
is often simply darkest, where if you keep your fire small

the cops aren't likely to come. As it's unlikely
these guys—if they can locate their money—
will find on aisle 6B that good Napa cabernet on sale
before suction-stepping their way back across the mud

to a nice burl of driftwood they'll straddle to drink
and discourse on the astounding chromatograph produced
by the sun's sliding down the back side of the world.
But who am I to say? Me here making another slice

by taking those men and, as we say, "using them,"
using the names I liked best—Mantegna, Ghirlandaio,
Pollaiuolo—though there were so many paintings
of Saint Sebastian's martyrdom to choose from, all

with some place in the background where the river goes
about its business and the hills are ripe with sheep.
Countryside that's lost on Saint Sebastian, who's already
tied up and arrowed through. But it's there

if you need it, if you want to tell yourself
another life is not so far away, just a few days
by donkey. And if, when you get there, the rocks
don't suit your taste, you'll find another landscape

right behind—another mountain, another river
falling one after another like old calendar pages.
Too pretty, their colors too perfect, these places
you would never believe in. But still you would go there.

The Salmon

Underneath the City

What are they doing down there but unsettling me,
swimming through that seamless dark:
passing into the culvert and under the boat shop,
under the Cadillac dealership with its ghost fins.
Under the backyard, under the parking lot
where milk trucks are bedded down with dogs; at night
electricity floods the wires above the chainlink.

And sometimes I study the garden's broken dirt
to detect the groundswell of their passage.
Or I walk out to the cedars where the culvert
feeds them back to Moxlie Creek. But so far,
nothing. Except one I saw leap
from the water in a perfect, frizzled crescent,
there where the stub of silver pipe ungutters

in the bay. The guy who'd hooked it
showed me the telltale black gums in its mouth,
after I'd watched him palm a rock and bring it down
hard on the skull, watched the fish relinquish
then sigh all its living out. That was weeks ago
and ever since I've listened for the wilderness
they make of their compulsion, of their one idea:

Against. Under the milk yard, where the dogs' chops
quiver, and the wires sing with what moves through
and makes them full (on rainy nights,
even the hardware glistens). And sometimes I find myself
stalled under a street lamp, snagged by the curb
like a yellow leaf. Crouched there to look
where a storm grate opens over these dark waters.

The Ghost Shirt

—*Museum of Natural History, NYC, 5/1/92,*
the first day of the riots

The blue whale swam through blue air in the basement
while upstairs the elephants twined together tusk by tusk,
and the enormous canoe was being rowed by the Tlingit

as they have rowed without moving for years through the dusk
in the Hall of the Americas. Empty space
was brocaded by schoolkids' shrieks

as teachers pantomimed in front of each glass case,
and I turned a corner and came up smack against the ghost shirt,
worn by a mannequin with no legs and no face—

                                  at first
it almost didn't register;
it was not what books had led me to expect: no beads
no ornament no chamois leather

or those shiny cornets made from rolled up snuff-tin lids.
Instead it was just a cotton shift
negotiating grimly between blue and green and red,

with some glyphs scrawled amateurishly across the breast
in ordinary pen: a thunderbird and some lightning,
a buffalo and its hoofprint,

one tree, one little man puffing
on a flume-sized pipe. Pentagram stars formed a cloud
atopside a smaller species of stippling

that I had to stare at a long time before I understood
meant bullets. Then I found myself checking for broken threads
to see if any of the holes were rimmed in blood—

but no: time or moths or bullets, it was anybody's guess.
A quote on the wall from the Paiute messiah
said *Indians who don't believe in the ghost dance*

will grow little, just about a foot high,
and stay that way. Then some of those
will be turned into wood and burned in fire—

and I left the museum wondering about which was worse:
to display a man's blood here
so every kid can practice crumpling as if falling off a horse

(& the kid knows exactly how to clutch the new air
entering his heart). Or to clean the shirt
as if the ghost blood had never been there.

***

This is the kind of story you could carry around
like a beaded key chain from a tourist trap:
how the ghost dance became a thunderstorm
that even summoning Buffalo Bill out
to the Standing Rock agency could not slake—
until the schoolhouses were empty
and the trading stores were empty
and the winter wheat went bony in the field

and the War Department had no idea what it meant
but that the Sioux had gone mad with their dancing
and that Yellow Bird wore a peculiar shirt when he chanted
Your bullets will not go toward us right before they did.

    ***

From the museum, I take the subway downtown
and change trains where the tunnels all converge
below Times Square, in one dank cavern underground

whose darkness seems so large it does not have edges.
Even at midafternoon, the shade there seethes
with people marching in a lockstep through that passage;

sometimes, when directed back over a shoulder, a mouth
on someone's profiled face will drop
and I'll see the tongue dart nervously along the teeth . . .

then the march becomes a gallop
when the walls begin to pound with an arriving train,
its riders rushing toward us in a yellowness crushed up

against the glass. And we board like cattle, one person
driving an elbow into another's gut
as we jam in (and we jam in . . .)

and coming up at Grand Central, I find it likewise knotted
with people ranged in single files,
shuffling toward the ticket counters in fits and stops

that give them time to paw the vast floor with their heels.
But what strikes me most is how loudly the silence
murmurs off the marble tiles

as if we were all underwater, hearing backward our own breath.
Then I remember that I bought a return on my way in
and hurry back down two flights of steps

to the lower level, where the train for Croton
sits almost full, though not scheduled to leave for half an hour
yet. Soon all the seats are gone

but the train keeps filling, arms and legs the mortar
in a wall of breasts and double-breasts. I avoid the gaze
and glare of those who hang on straps over

my head, and it isn't until the train begins to wheeze
from its hydraulics and slowly labors
past the gate that everyone around me will unfreeze

enough to speak: about a city bus and its passengers
rocked onto its flank and set aflame, a hundred black
and Spanish kids aswarm with Molotovs and crowbars . . .

which is the story we sow along the darkness, until the track
rises into daylight above Ninety-seventh Street,
where the broken windows have been boarded back

with plywood, each painted with its own domestic scene
—curtains gathered primly or potted geraniums on the sills—
though otherwise, everything looks to me as it has always been,

with the same nimbuses of spray paint on the trestles,
the alphabet stuffed like heavy furniture
reciting its addition on the same brick walls

. . . until we cross the East River
where everybody lets their breath go with relief,
the wheels droning their steady whuckerwhuckerwhucker

as the train settles into its top speed
and we skitter along the Hudson, where nothing is except
water on one side, on the other side a ravine

overstudded with junk: a Cadillac sunk axle-
deep a shopping cart the front wheels of a stroller
menacingly airborne like the forelegs of *Tyrannosaurus rex*—

and it's here the train zippers
to an abrupt stop (though we haven't come to any station),
steeping us anxiously awhile in quiet, until the whispers

blossom like umbrellas opening before the rain:
first *they're blocking the engine* then *they're lying down
on the tracks*, rumors that ripple through the train

like a wave sweeping upstream, then back down,
by which time the muttering has escalated to a shout
that goes *Keep going!* and *We've got to run those fuckers down!*

    ***

Between the train and whoever lies down in its path,
you could say there's a ghost shirt,
whatever it is that makes the locomotive stop
if the engineer can see far enough ahead.
I think it is a dotted line
looping the outskirts of our being human—
ghostly because of the ease with which
its perforations can be ripped. Also
because the sole proof of its presence

lies in the number of days we go unhurt,
a staggering number, especially when you consider
how much bigger the world is than a train.
And how something even as small as a bullet
can pick out of elsewhere's 359 degrees
one shape, and suddenly everything is changed,
though the calx of what didn't happen
remains in curiously enduring traces
like the stone casts that larval caddis flies
leave behind them in the stream
(& *larvae:* from the latin word for ghost).
What you have is always less
a history of a people, any people,
than a history of its rocks: first a heap
then a cathedral and soon a heap again,
while the names get amortized like money.
Like Damian Williams, the one they called Football,
who held his bloody cinderblock aloft
and danced as if he were stomping out a hundred
baby flames: Rodney King, Reginald Denny,
William Cody, Stacey Koon. And Black Coyote,
who refused to give up his Winchester
after Yellow Bird danced the first few steps
before Colonel Forsythe's pony soldiers
broke all hell loose. And Black Coyote,
whom Turning Hawk said was crazy,
"a young man of bad influence and in fact a nobody."

    ***

I want to say that we weren't all white on that train,
but mostly we were—
and when without explanation the engine started up again,

those who weren't fell away to the edge of the herd
and got off where the conductor squawked out *Spuyten Duyvil,*
Marblehead and *Yonkers* . . .

and as we rolled I strained to imagine the sound a wheel
would make as it milled through someone's ribs,
listening for them bedded down in every mile

until I got off way out in the suburbs.
From the station I called my father to come pick me up
and waited for him half-hidden in some shrubs

so that when he arrived I could make my usual leap
into his Mercedes so no one sees me getting in.
I remember what it was like in that town, growing up

so out of it I didn't even see the affluence back then—
and how we kids rolled our eyes whenever our parents
started in on the WPA and the Great Depression

and being glad for a day's honest work even if that meant
no more than laying a stone and piling another on top
—part of a war we waged in serial installments,

mostly over what we put on our backs, or feet, or not:
the tattered clothes we wore to ape a poverty
about which our folks claimed we did not know shit

(though like every kid in that town I toted around my copy
of a gospel that one week was *Soul on Ice*
and the next week *Bury My Heart at Wounded Knee*)

—which maybe explains why it still makes me nervous,
though twenty years have passed: to be riding around in a car
that cost more than, elsewhere, someone's house,

while I'm trying to explain to my old father
what it meant to me to see the ghost shirt
just before Wall Street shut down and every broker

fled. And not just fled, but reverted,
as if what made us human had been only a temporary crust
on our skins, as if there were no way to stop the backward

march into the swamp. Pretty soon we'd all be just
like rats but bigger, and combat ready . . .
but here again my father claimed I didn't know whereof

I spoke: all day the television had showed the city
eerily at peace. And the only fires were the tiny flames
of people holding candles, outside the public library.

Notes

The poem "Kilned" contains an epigraph from the sculptor Stephen Lang, who works with molten lava on Hawaii's Big Island. The quote comes from an article on Lang that appeared in *Omni* magazine.

"Beige Trash" is dedicated to my friend the poet Rodney Jones.

"Foley" refers to the enhancing of sound during a film's post-production, so named for Jack Foley, once head of sound effects at Universal Studios, who in the 1930s simulated Niagara Falls by spraying a tin sign with a hose. Though it is a widely recounted bit of trivia that Andy Williams dubbed Lauren Bacall's singing in *To Have and Have Not*, actually Bacall ended up lip-syncing to her own voice. Thus the end result is a simulation of something authentic that is nonetheless commonly perceived to be a fake.

"Serotonin" originally appeared in a chapbook for the poet Philip Booth, under whom I studied in the eighties. The poem is dedicated to him and to my workshop-mates: Jane, Chris, Ken.

"The Ghost Shirt" uses fragments from Dee Brown's *Bury My Heart at Wounded Knee*.

Finally, I want to thank George Saunders and Dan Menaker for making this book happen. Also James Rudy for being my research assistant, housekeeper, cook, paddling buddy and all-around Sherpa these past ten years, through thin and thinner. *Nunc scio quid sit Amor.*

LUCIA PERILLO has published two previous collections: *The Body Mutinies*, which won several awards, including the Revson Prize from PEN, and *Dangerous Life*, which received the Norma Farber Award from the Poetry Society of America. Her poems have appeared in such magazines as *The Atlantic* and *The Kenyon Review*, and they have been included in the *Pushcart* and the *Best American Poetry* anthologies. A former park ranger, she now teaches at Southern Illinois University in Carbondale.

ABOUT THE TYPE

This book was set in Centaur, a typeface designed by the American
typographer Bruce Rogers in 1929. Centaur was a typeface that
Rogers adapted from the fifteenth-century type of Nicolas Jenson
and modified in 1948 for a cutting by the Monotype Corporation.